RUNIC STATES

THE
SHAMANIC
PERCEPTION
OF
QUANTUM
REALITIES

BY
KEVIN STEFFEN

Copyright © 1995
by
Kevin Steffen

ISBN 1-57353-108-1

EPB-AW-108
an
ESCHATON BOOK
from

PRODUCTIONS, INC

60 East Chestnut Street, #236
Chicago, IL 60611

RUNIC STATES

TABLE OF CONTENTS

PREFACE ix

Chapter 1: Runes Today 1

    Hokey religion or quantum cosmology 1

    The psyche's connection: symbolism and systems 2

Chapter 2: A Runic History 7

    Just the facts 7

    Fantasies and other speculative thinking 15

    Personally speaking 17

Chapter 3: The Individual Runes 19

    WYRD -   - The rune that isn't there 20

    FEHU - ᚠ   - The big bang 25

    URUZ - ᚢ   - Uncovering your strengths 29

    THURISAR - ᚦ   - The thunder speaks 33

    ANSUR - ᚨ   - Intellect and inspiration or... 37

    RAIDHO - ᚱ   - As the wheel turns 41

    KENAZ - ᚲ   - Into the fire 44

    GEBO - ᚷ   - The sum of the heart 47

    WUNJO - ᚹ   - The banner of the clan 49

    HAEGEL - ᚺ   - Shipwrecked in the storm 52

NAUDHIR - ↑	- When the need is great	56
ISA - I	- The stillness of ice	60
JERA - ≷	- Because you deserve it	64
EIHWAR - ↕	- The tree of communication	69
PERTHO - ⌇	- When life is a gamble	73
ELHAR - Y	- The buffalo of the north	77
SOWHILO - ⚡	- Bask in the son shine	80
TIWAR - ↑	- Trials and tribulations	83
BERKANO - ß	- Within life, the Goddess	86
EHWAR - ᛖ	- The ears of the horse	90
MANNAZ - ᛗ	- The clan of mankind	93
LAGUR - ſ	- The drink of the Gods	95
ING - ◊	- The forgotten God	98
DAGAZ - ᛞ	- The end ... or the beginning	102
OTHALA - ⋈	- The house of the clan	105

Chapter 4: Systems and Structures 111

    Runes, numbers, and other aspects 111

    The family grouping system 119

Chapter 5: Tools 131

    Rune Flashcards 131

    Rune Sets 131

Rune Board	132
Rune Table	133
Bind Runes	133
Rune Wand	139
Chapter 6: Techniques	**143**
Carving Runes	143
The Rune Reading	144
Writing with Runes	147
Chapter 7: Der Wikinger	**151**
A Historic Rune Game	151
Chapter 8: The Roots of Magic	**155**
Physics, Quantum Physics, and Metaphysics	155
Masters of Spirit Magic	159
The Magic in Song	162
BIBLIOGRAPHY	**167**
GLOSSARY	**171**
INDEX	**175**

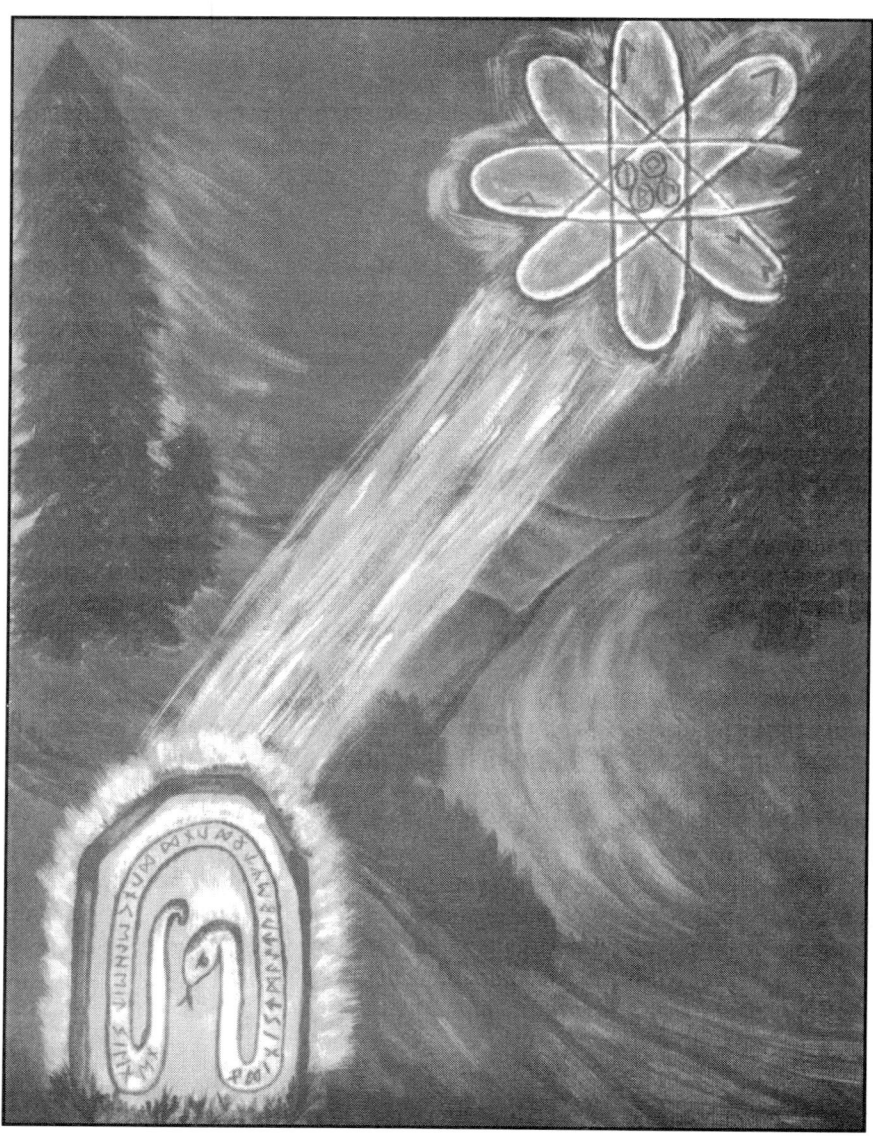

The author's vision, which inspired this book.

PREFACE

Most books on the runes are either written from a linguistic point of view looking at the runes as little more than an alphabet, or they approach the use of the runes from the religious and mystical side, concentrating on the symbology. The texts by R. I. Page fall in the first category, while the texts by Edred Thorsson and Ralph Blum fall into the second. I would like to thank and acknowledge all three of these authors for the work they have done in keeping the knowledge of the runes alive.

The cosmology of a person is the way that person thinks about the cosmos, its relations and its interactions with the individual. This is just a bit more all encompassing than the world view concept in literature and psychology since it also includes the religion and the internal aspects of the person's psyche.

This book is about the runes and how they can fit into the cosmologies of people today. To do this it is necessary to examine the cosmologies of the cultures that used the runes in the past. In this endeavor we will cover aspects of linguistics, psychology, anthropology, theology, and physics, covering a broader scope than most other books on the runes. The end result desired is to show you how the runes can be the symbols in a language you can use in working with your subconscious, fitting them into your cosmology you use in dealing with the events in your life.

The runes are more like a computer language than a language spoken by people. The runes are the symbols or syntax of the language, but the structure that forms the rules of how the symbols are to be used is provided by your cosmology and your subconscious. In other words, the rules are completely subjective and change slightly for each individual.

To help with your understanding of the symbology in each rune Silver Crow has created a mandala for each rune for those more visually oriented. She also deserves thanks for the wonderful work she did on the other illustrations showing the Eddic universe and runic symbology.

Finally, as pointed out later, the Germanic tribes believed the fates work behind the scenes of reality to bring the pattern into being. Thus, Kapitan Schaus and I were drawn together to work on bringing back DER WIKINGER, and the runic ring of a Viking chieftain. As I worked on the draft of this book he supplied me with a cast of the ring, with the plans for DER WIKINGER, and with other information from his trips back to Germany and Northern Europe. For his assistance I must thank him and the fates which set us working together.

One note on chronology: Many of the people using runes wish to use dating systems based on their religious beliefs, not Christianity. Instead of confusing those who do not, the dates are given in the form of ce and bce which do not require any conversion. Refer to the glossary for the definitions of these terms.

RUNIC STATES

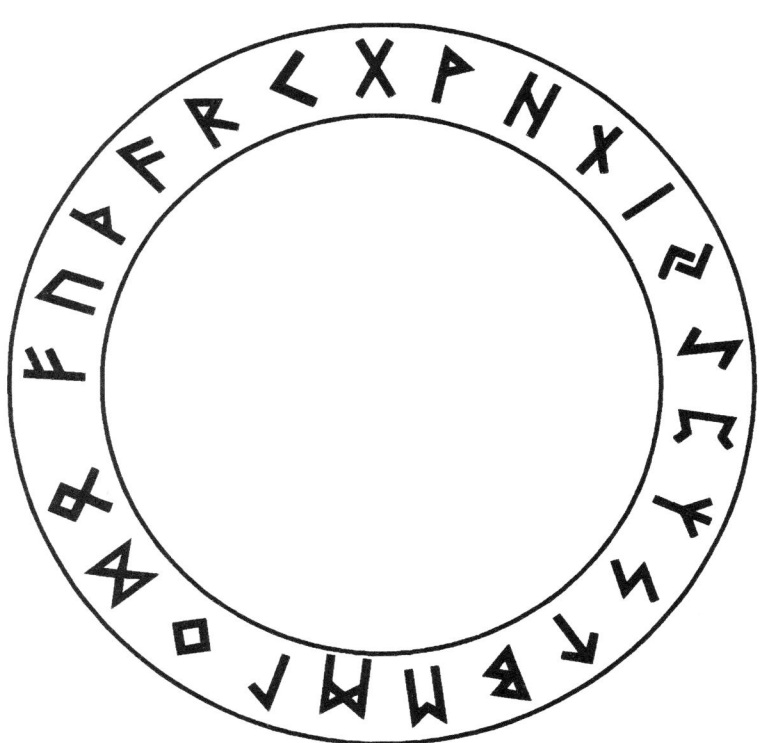

RUNIC STATES

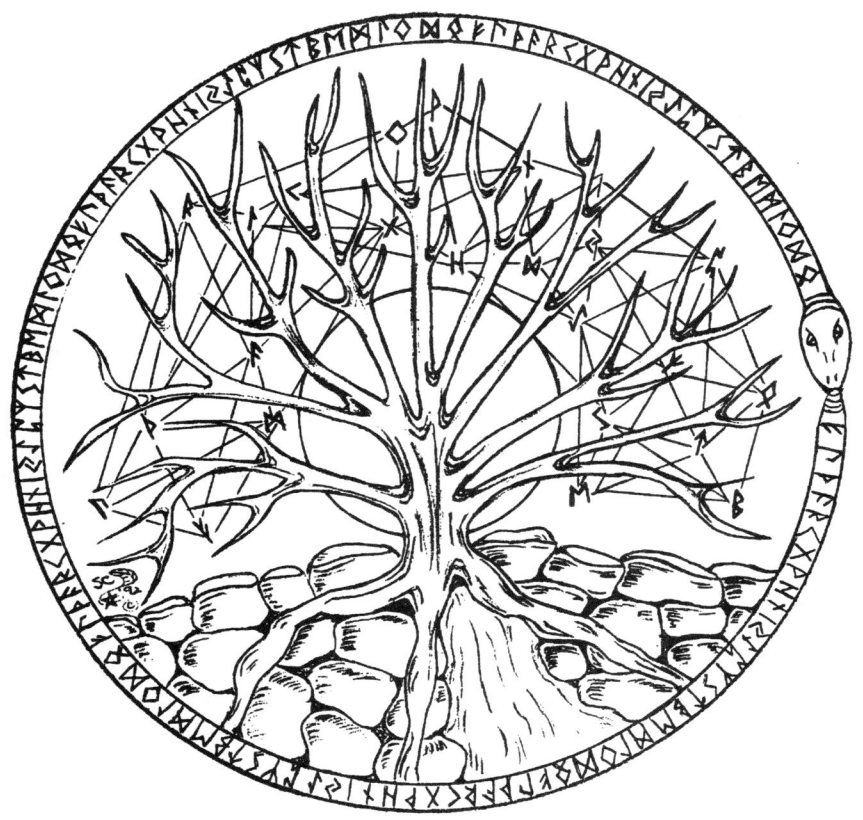

Chapter 1: RUNES TODAY

HOKEY RELIGION OR QUANTUM COSMOLOGY?

We will start this discussion of Runes with a reference to the box office hit STAR WARS where Han Solo quips *Hokey religions and ancient weapons are no match for a good blaster...* This is a suitable quote for starting the book for many reasons. The first one to be covered is simply that it shows the prevailing attitude of Western man since the age of reason: Religion is dead or dying and science is replacing it.

Second, some people consider myths and all other remnants of knowledge that "have not withstood the test of time" as hokey religions or silly superstitions. They imply that there was no truth to the ideas or they would still be widely accepted. However, as Han Solo pointed out - - an idea and dated technology can be militarily defeated by force of numbers or technological superiority on the battlefield. This is especially true if the knowledge is not universally transmitted to all members of the culture or if the conquerors are ruthless enough to get away with genocide; or in the modern euphemism from Bosnia, cultural cleansing.

This first chapter will cover the methodology and background information on the approach taken to study the runes in the light of modern science and quantum physics. How, and why the runes are as applicable today in dealing with the symbolism of the human psyche as they were 1400 years ago.

A northern Europe creation myth starts *In the beginning there was fire* (KENAZ - <) *and ice* (ISA - I). KENAZ - < and ISA - I being two of the elder rune set. A physical chemistry text categorizes reactions into two classes endothermic, taking heat from the surroundings, (ISA - I) and exothermic, giving heat to the surroundings, (KENAZ - <). Quantum theory in physics states the electrons in the atom will show both wave properties (LAGUR - ᚱ) and particle properties (ISA - I).

Runes are being used and studied today from several angles. As a religious tool, the runes are being used by people examining their heritage of northern European religions. They are being used as foci in meditation through their sonic connections. They are used as a divinatory tool because of their connection with daily living situations. Finally, the movie and entertainment industries are using runes as stage props when an exotic alphabet is wanted.

These various uses of runes are possible due to their being linked to mankind's body, mind, and spiritual levels of being in the early history of writing. It is the runes' everyday use by these people and the symbology they placed in them that I feel is most pertinent to us today. As dream symbology can be used to explore your psyche, so can the runes. As the symbology of the Tarot is valid today, so is that of the runes. As physics and chemistry are used to describe the world we live in, so can the runes be used.

A hokey religion? Some people will say the runes are a product of the devil and will denounce them as a false religion no matter what the facts are. The debunkers have a marvelous gift for ignoring any facts which contradict their thoughts or threaten their limited world view.

A quantum cosmology? Definitely so since some of the runes can be linked to the physical states and conditions found in the world.

THE PSYCHE'S CONNECTION: SYMBOLISM AND SYSTEMS

Anthropologists, psychologists, and behaviorists have a common factor. They have all completed studies in their own specialties to demonstrate that people do not, indeed they can not handle speech, abstract thought, or respond to the environment directly on either a conscious or on an unconscious level; but that the brain processes all stimuli as symbols. The only direct response to stimuli is that which never reaches the brain's cortex such as the flinch reaction to pain which only goes to the brain's stem. You've already withdrawn the hand you've burned before you can say "OUCH!" In *Language: Mirror, Tool and Weapon* this is expanded on in saying that it is not possible to think a thought that your language does not have words (symbols) or structure to handle.

How does this apply to runes? Runes are symbols, thus they can be manipulated or used by both the conscious and subconscious to cope with the environment. Runes as a group of symbols can be thought of as the words in a language. A language also has a structure or rules in addition to the symbols which govern manipulation of the symbols.

The structure or order of the runes derives from the meanings ascribed to the runic symbols and the rules of manipulation from the culture and world view of the person using the runes. Thus, the runes can be used by anyone comfortable with the symbols and their meanings. The rules of manipulation are mutable, open to individualization, just in the same way that language is susceptible to having regional dialects. Every person develops a unique way of talking; a speech, tone and voice pattern that no one else can mimic with 100% accuracy. Working with runes is subject to this same effect of your personality and the psyche, so you will develop a unique style in dealing with the runes. Anyone who desires and puts forth the effort can learn another language with a personal style of a dialect coming with fluency. If you are comfortable with the runes as a set of symbols there is no reason you cannot learn to speak the language of the runes.

As an example, Ralph Blum sees the symbolism of the runes as limited to stages in the cycles of life. The rules and structure he uses is that of the Christian religion. The runes have no religious meaning of their own in his view. Edred Thorsson on the other hand allows the symbols to have meanings pertaining to procreation, living, and the various Gods and Goddesses of the Norse pantheon. The structure is also based on the Norse religion while his rules are based on magic and the ancient Norse world view.

As you consciously work with the runes, your unconscious and subconscious have access to the rune's symbolism. This is the psyche's connection to the runes. As your psyche works with these new symbols, it will personalize the symbols over time, as you discover interrelationships between the runes, a system and structure in the runes. As you meditate on a rune you may get a flash of shape and sound, a complete understanding of the view of where the rune receives its shape and meaning, or several meanings. This is an upwelling of information from the subconscious.

Every month or so someone advertises having **the** diet to make you thin and happy. They expound on **the new definitive** book on runes or any other topic you may pick. Or they talk about the only **true** path for enlightened people to follow.

There is a story that is attributed to everyone from Buddha to Confucius to a Tao master. The Buddha version goes something like this:

One disciple came to the Buddha and begged for enlightenment.

"Master," he said, "You teach us that the way to Satori is to follow the eight fold path yet you treat each of us differently. Is not the eight fold path the same for everyone?"

3

"It is not," Buddha replied.

"Then how many paths to Satori are there?" the disciple asked.

"How many people are there?" Buddha queried in answer.

There are many different morals to that story. The point that I wanted to make here is this: When dealing with the runes in your psyche, you must ask the right question to receive the answer you want, that is, you must ask the right question to receive the answer most appropriate to your situation. Phrasing is important, slightly different questions may give vastly different answers.

When working with systems as an engineer you learn that you can almost never do anything to the system with impunity. If you tweak a Thing-a-ma-bob in front of you, the Doohickey on your left and the What-cha-ma-callit way out yonder on your right may be affected. Humanity and every society humanity creates is a system. The psychologists know this, but often overlook it since systems analysis is not a required part of their field of study. Whenever you do something or say something, especially when dealing with a symbology, one person may be offended while someone else may receive an insight of the **EUREKA!!!** magnitude.

This is all due to the structure they have in their conscious and subconscious. The runes are the **symbols.** Your beliefs make the **structure** the symbols are placed into, and the **rules** for using the symbols. You will find slightly different meaning interpreting a runecast than I will in reading the same runecast. It does not mean either of us is wrong. As Einstein proved: everything is relative. Two observers cannot view the same event at the same time because they cannot be in the same space at the same time. Therefore the event has changed due to the space and time separating the viewers. As you work with the runes, you will make your connection to them, and have your favorite meaning for each rune.

As the title suggests, the topic of this section was really about you, the way you think, the way you react to stimuli. When you work with the runes, your psyche will have a new language to speak in, a new way of writing. A word of warning here at the beginning. Your psyche will redefine the symbols in the runes to match your world view. If all the runes are seen as concerning one topic, be it sex, or power, or any one topic, it could possibly identify a fixation and the runes will be useless until the fixation is resolved. Yet it is beneficial to have several runes with similar meanings so there is more than one view on the subject the runes are covering. This is the basis of the system covered in this book, a symbolic construct that is capable of serving as a direct language between your conscious and subconscious.

Meditate on one rune for a week to a month, and you will begin to discover it where you live, inside you. It will begin to resonate in your psyche. Then you will be able to notice slight changes in the emphasis of the rune if you watch closely during the time. You may also notice that it has been working in your life for a while, or that it starts appearing as you meditate on it.

RUNIC STATES

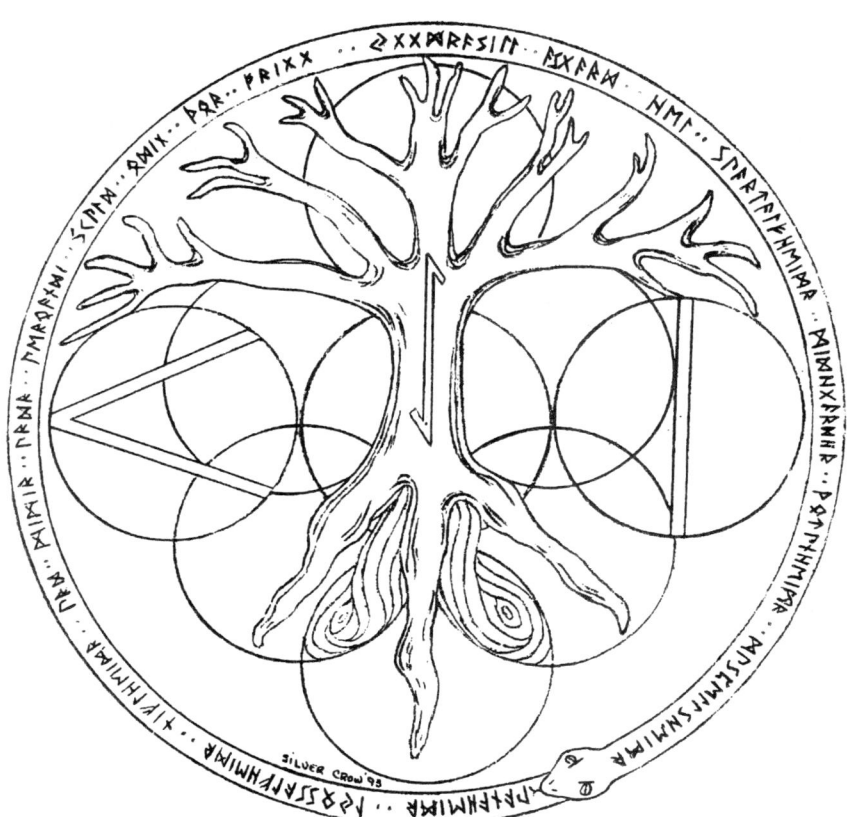

Chapter 2: A RUNIC HISTORY

JUST THE FACTS

R. I. Page, a Cambridge linguist, wrote a book titled *Reading the Past: RUNES*. The good professor calls the belief of a magical property to the runes highly imaginative speculation and escapist theorization. Yet he acknowledges that the interpretation of almost any inscription will have as many different meanings as rune scholars who interpret it, because many of the inscriptions have magical gibberish included.

By accepted definition, runes are the alphabet of the Germanic tribes covering a territory from Rumania to the British Isles and France to northernmost Scandinavia. The many different Futharks or alphabets are the result of changing languages and pronunciation in the same language. The runes are specifically designed for carving in wood, straight vertical lines cut across the grain, as do the diagonal lines. There are no horizontal bars or cuts to hide in the grain of the wood.

The earliest surviving inscriptions are from 200 ce, already well dispersed, therefore probably at least 100 to 400 years old by that time. This dating would preclude the necessity of having a pictograph history. The tribes' usage of runes began to decline in areas with the conversion to Christianity around 1100 to 1200 ce when the Christian church's Roman alphabet became prominent. However, the church at this time did not proscribe the earlier runic alphabet, and even allowed runic inscriptions in the church and graveyard. These runic inscriptions are prayers and stories of Christianity set in the language and runic alphabet of the people of the area. This began to change in 500 to 700 years with the religious persecutions of the later bishops and popes.

If you consider the runes as a simple alphabet, there is no need for the blank rune, the WYRD. The prevalence of magical and religious carvings show there was more to the runes than just a mundane alphabet, just as the Cabala shows the spiritual esoteric meanings to the Jewish and Christian scholars placed in the Roman and Jewish alphabets. With the earliest time of surviving inscriptions being at 200 ce, this means the time is beyond that where pictographic or ideographic writing is normal or even mandatory for consideration. However, there is no evidence as to how much earlier the runes were in use since the wood on which most inscriptions were made rotted away.

There is a maxim that form follows function given materials and tools available. In other words, the design of an article reflects the world of the people who created it. Form and function are interdependent, and vary with the tools and material that are used to create the article.

As an example visualize each of the following writings: a fine calligraphy quill on vellum, a ball point pen on bond paper, movable type as in newspapers, the output of a laser printer from a computer. Each can have the same sentence, but each will have a totally different look and impact on the reader.

The next factor of change is that of culture. The more free time a culture has, the greater chance of being stylized or embellished. To stay with writing: the test of a clerk or scribe was could he write and be read, a noble was expected to have a pretty handwriting if he could write at all, but a monk's writing was a veritable calligrapher's dream with enough curls to make Marie Antoinette's hairdresser jealous. However, with the disdain and vehement attacks of the Puritan preachers on the frippery and finery of the day, men lost the ability to wear silks, satin, and lace while writing lost the flair and curls of the time, becoming more stylized straight lines and circular arcs by the time of the American Revolution in the late 1700's.

The collection of the Finnish creation songs/stories is the Kalevala. The individual songs or runots (rune notes?) in Finnish were not collected as a homogeneous collection and written down until the early 1800s by Elias Lonnrot by 1835 he had collected 32, and by 1849 he had almost 64. Ursula Synge retold the verses as stories in the tradition of the Greek and Roman myths in *Land of Heroes A Retelling of the Kalevala*.

With the runes we know a sound of the language was associated with each rune. It is the starting sound of the rune's name as R. I. Page pointed out in his book. However, as in the Tibetan bells, the tone of the rune is lost when moved from an oral to a written tradition. Hence the rune note would be lost while the rune sound remains. While this may seem to belong in the next section on speculation, the runes were used in the area of the world inhabited by the Finnish tribes, where intonation of words is important in both song and language.

In *Kalevala The Land of the Heroes* W. F. Kirby translates Lonnrot's collection in the same form as the epics as told by Lonnrot. The preface tells of the gathering and compiling of the songs from the east of Finland and the northwest of Russia. Even in the mid 1800's there was identification of the path of the players in the Kalevala from Shaman to God/dess to Hero/ine to Christian Devil. Much of the change discussed occurred between 800 and 1200 ce during the times of the Vikings. This is also the pinnacle of the runes in use. The end for both the runes and the Finnish sagas began around 1100 ce when Christianity conquered the region.

In this reference to Odhin as a shaman, as well as the heroes of the Kalevala, there are further connections to be followed later in the book. The definition and duties of the shaman as well as a portion of a chapter listing ways the stories of Odhin describe the activities of a shaman can be found in another reference, *Shamanism Archaic Techniques of Ecstasy.* Here Mircea Eliade devotes over 500 pages to define the parameters of shamanism with references to almost as many books in the footnotes and bibliography.

In the section on TIWAR - ↑ there is a short mention of *The Old Norse Sagas* where Halvdan Koht lectured in 1929 that there was no historical evidence for trial by combat, just statements in romantic sagas. Where do his lectures to our grandfathers (at that time most colleges did not allow women to attend) in college fit in the study of runes? Much of the use of runes must be drawn from inference or recovered by trial and error since there are no instruction manuals from 800 ce on using runes.

The Norse Sagas were in reality sagas of Iceland, being told by the Saga tellers of Iceland. Originally, during the time the runes were in use, the Vikings of Denmark and Norway were the ones to settle Iceland, then Greenland, and finally Lief Erickson found Vineland (North America) leaving runes in New England, which are accepted as historical, and a marker in the Kennsington, Minnesota which is of disputed authenticity according to some experts for lack of corroborating evidence.

Some experts debunk the Kennsington stele which tells of a Viking trading expedition's exploits in the area. They never heard of, or refuse to accept an archeological project's findings from 1967. The project was using infrared photography to map Native American camps on the banks of the Missouri river 22 miles from Pierre, South Dakota. At the site on the river they found the patterns of an encampment they were looking for. Immediately next to it was the remnants of the bastions and other fortifications with pilings of a 200 foot spacing in a pattern typical of Norse fortifications circa 1362 ce. This is exactly the same sort of evidence that is accepted for the Vineland site by the same experts.

The exploits of these early settlers and explorers were told at the guesting table. In Iceland, the tellers became skilled in telling an exciting tale where the listeners were given insight to the motivations of the participants without the gross manipulations of today's psychological thrillers.

This oral tradition and the demise of the use of runes began to peak around 1000 ce. At that time, the church bishops and the royalty began the written sagas which quickly changed into romantic stories and political/religious propaganda within 200 years. At the height of the popularity of the saga, the kings of Norway and Denmark hired Icelandic saga men to tell their stories. Though cousins, the rivalry between the Danish and Norwegian kings can be seen in the slant of the sagas, each calling the other barbarian pagan sorcerers, needing the light of Christianity, while in reality, both were kingdoms founded by Christian kings.

In these sagas, Halvdan Koht finds and remarks on the multiplicity of three. The magical use of this number was so ingrained in the psyche of the people that it formed a portion of their legal system. Two examples being a set fine of three marks for a penalty, and the term of outlawry being set at three years. He further points out that it was believed that it took three repetitions to close out a cycle, two failures or ventures of limited success before full success the third time. Have you ever heard the saying "If at first you don't succeed, try, try again."? This multiplicity of three even extends to the Finnish Kalevala, far distant in time and space from Iceland.

Finally, we will get back to what we started with. Halvdan studied the legal systems, court cases, and laws relating to these times. These people loved the vicarious thrills of lawsuits. It was new and more rewarding than betting on chess matches. It was a game with very strict rules. If you could trick your opponent into violating the rules, you automatically won your lawsuit, and the object of the suit, be it a farm or a fine, or other merchandise. Like "The People's Court" of today, it was a vicarious thrill to listen to the scandals of the neighbors.

Halvdan maintains he found no trace of any lawsuit being settled by combat. Most of the incidents of reports of trial by combat occurred a couple hundred years earlier, but there were still no records of such a trial. He concludes that these false reports may have been the fabrication of the bishops to discredit the practice of the earlier pagan times. After all, if the ownership of a farm was decided by a duel, all the brothers who had claim to the land could sue the victor and new owner of the farm to get their farm back.

However, he also points out that insult or injury could be settled with a murder or a duel. So supposedly, if someone slandered your good name, you could sue him, or attack him physically, settling it in blood. Many of the sagas dealt with how an insult or other injury was settled with a duel or vengeance, many times sparking a feud. Whether you allow the existence of a trial by combat depends on whether you are speaking literally or figuratively. Literally, the law did not allow for a trial by combat, but the practice was to settle the dispute either by a lawsuit, or by a duel. Combat and lawsuits were like the two sides of a coin. Flip it, after all, life is just a game of chance.

So far, we have skipped around a wide geographic area, just as the runes were found, following the runes as a form of writing. To tie these facts together a bit, now we get into a time line following not the spread of the runes, but the tribes who used them over a thousand years.

Starting with 200 ce we find the first remains of runes carved on wood preserved on the continent. This signals the arrival of at least a vanguard of the Germanic tribes. Historically, the Saxons were among the Germanic tribes that invaded the British Isles in 400's and 500's. Once settled, those that invaded were called Anglo-Saxons to distinguish them from the tribes that stayed on the mainland. Some of the other tribes on the mainland went into the northern reaches of the continent becoming what we know now as Norse, Finns, Swedes, and Danes. These tribes are collectively referred to in the popular press as Vikings.

For approximately 300 years, the tribes on the continent were busy filling all the available land. They built farms, towns, and raided among themselves. There is evidence of these tribes trading as far as the middle east and Mediterranean sea thanks to the ships they built.

There is a preponderance of materials not native to the area found at the sites of Viking towns. This included glass and silver coins from all over the Mediterranean. You see, there is no silver ore in the Scandinavian area, though iron is the most common ore.

When the available land began to run out, they emigrated. Small groups of the tribes from the north took holdings on the isles, mainly staying to coastal regions. A map of England shows the most Scandinavian names on the Northeast of England with a few on the southwest coast. A lot of these settlements were peaceful, making use of lands that the Anglo-Saxons had no use for. Of course, sometimes people objected to new people coming in and taking land to live on.

Between 780 and 1000 ce the Viking raids took place. Some people record the first raid being when a local lord tried to force a shipload of these Northmen to court. Needless to say, the freedom loving Northmen took exception to this. The score of the resulting melee could be stated Vikings 40, Saxons 0.

The majority of the settlements dated from 875 to 902 ce. It was at this same time many Vikings became raiders, having a great time looting monasteries, convents, and any other place where riches were easy pickings. In a way, these raids actually helped the advancement of the British Isles, forcing them to develop walled cities and mutual defense pacts between neighboring lords. Remember, the legend of King Arthur hints that he spent more time fighting the Norse raiders than anything until he united the lords of England so they would defend each other when attacked.

Around 961, some of the Northmen decided to settle in France. They had such a monumental success terrorizing the locals that they were given the entire area of Normandy as a bribe to leave the rest of France alone. There are records of similar bribes being paid by the Anglo-Saxon lords to the Danes. In so doing, this act became known as a Danegeld.

In 1066 William of the Normans took most of England, earning the name William the Conqueror. Just another example of the broad expansion force of the Germanic tribes. While the last of the massive raids of the Northmen happened about sixty years earlier, this was the last of the major raids utilizing the Dragon ships of the Vikings.

In the popular press, the entire group of invaders from 780 to 1000 are lumped together as Viking raiders, no matter where they originated from. Depending upon the source of the document, these folk were called Danes, Heathen, Northmen, Viking, and a couple of other less than complimentary names. In the 900 years since the raids, invasions, and settlements of the British Isles ended, the technically pure Anglo-Saxon have bred themselves out of existence by marrying the Vikings and the Norman conquerors. Anyone of caucasian race with the exception of the Irish and Scottish coming from Great Britain is tarred with the same brush, and referred to as Anglo-Saxon in the popular press.

Previously, I introduced the anthropological and sociological maxim of how a tool's function determines its shape, and given the local availability, the material it is made of. There is a new technique which utilizes this concept called reverse engineering being used by computer wizards and by archaeologists. By studying the shape and structure of a tool, we determine its use, or its manufacture, or the psychology of the people who created it.

This brings us back to the subject of the Viking's long ship, and the men who sailed them. The basic principle by which all ships are built is that of displacement. In order to float, the ship must push aside or displace more water than it weighs. This can be done in two main ways. You can build it long, low, and wide like a canoe as was the Viking long ship, or you can make it taller and shorter as the Romans did, and hence the later Anglo-Saxons of Great Britain.

The long ship has its advantages. With a shallow draft, it does not need as much water to float in as the taller tubs, and could sail closer to the shore, and actually unload or load at a reasonably sandy beach without a wharf or pier to tie up to. It is also more maneuverable in heavy seas, and more likely to survive rough water without sinking.

This design also has a few drawbacks. Unlike the taller ships, there is not room for a below deck. The deck is merely a flat place to stand so you do not have to trip over the ribs of the ship. This means the Vikings could not store all the goods below the deck, and have room for cabins or sleeping hammocks or other such amenities as the other sailors enjoyed. If a wave did wash in, this also meant that it did not just wash over the deck and off other side, but could fill the hull. Then it was a case of bail or sink.

The inherent greatness of this design, and the toughness of the men who sailed these ships is paid testament to in the wide area they covered in trade. Over two hundred years before Columbus journeyed across the sea, the Vikings landed in Vineland on the North American shores. Still many years before that journey, they traded from the North Sea to the Mediterranean Sea, and very probably went further south, though no Runic remains were found farther to the South such as in Africa.

Built low, long, and wide, these ships were just the vehicle for a man who wanted a fast trip with a heavy cargo that was not too bulky. These men would not be interested in bales of cotton or wool, but more so in the bolts of cloth made from them. These ships were not ore barges, but rather carried the gold and tin and silver articles fashioned from the ore.

Finally, we can get down to the psychological or cultural analysis that is derived from the engineering observations above which affect our study of the runes. Unlike many of ships that sailed the seas from the time of Cleopatra's party boat, the long ship did not have decking and enclosed cabins for the captain or the crew. I will tentatively state two conclusions for this. First, unlike the Roman ships and late Anglo-Saxon (also called English) ships, the Viking captain did not consider himself a class above the crew. Since the crew had no hard shelter, the captain would not also. This is a mark of a true leader, not some martinet ruling by fear or a false sense of superiority and craving superior luxuries to his men.

Second, if the weather was so foul you could not sleep in an open boat, then you should not be sleeping anyway. The Viking was not afraid of a little foul weather, and preferred to look whatever was coming straight in the face. He did not hide below decks. The *Edda* which tells of the actions of the Gods and Goddesses, does not leave room to be fatalistic about your fate or wyrd or geas.

Steered by a long paddle mounted on a gimbal on the right side, the Viking ship was very much like a canoe with up to forty oars in the water as well as a sail. Like a modern sailboat, the sail could be raised and lowered with a block and tackle. When lowered, the sail could be tied or reefed to the yard, and the yard rotated so it rested on supports running fore and aft. This was vital for foul weather, and reflected in the shape of the rune NAUDHIR - ᚾ.

A few definitions may be needed here. The mast is the upright pole that supports the sail. It is stepped into a special slot which is like a reinforced boot rising from the keel, where it is wedged into place. Some drawings of Viking longships show the mast reinforced by lines running to the sides as well as fore and aft known as stays. If placed in the wrong position, stays limit the action and swing of the sail. The illustrations with the sail reefed on the supports while the ship is being propelled by oars mainly do not show the stays. The fore and aft stays if shown are attached to the deck in front and rear respectively.

The sail is attached at the top to a yard which was raised and lowered by a block and tackle at the top of the mast. The set of the sail would be maintained by two sheets, (or ropes for the landlubbers) attached to the bottom corners of the sail. According to one source it was possible to reef the sail, or shorten the amount of sail open by tying it to the yard for high winds without lashing it down altogether and using oars only. The Oseberg ship has a removable boom to allow tacking and sailing almost straight upwind, as well as a net to cover and reinforce the sail.

Unlike the Roman Galleys which were similar in having sail and oars, the sailors on the long boats sat on their sea chests instead of benches to row. When coming into a hostile port, or attacking another ship, the sailor's shields could be fastened to the side of the ship to give them more protection against arrows and other projectiles. Trading was a dangerous business back then. The trader who did not defend what he had soon had nothing, not even his life.

Very little is written about these sailors except as barbarian raiders of the civilized world. Like the modern news shows of today, there is not much news to write about fishermen or honest traders, but thieves and pirates are worth noting and complaining about. Not all the Northmen were raiders all the time. There were peaceful trading ships that supplemented their income by raiding coasts that did not wish to trade. There is documentation for the Vikings having peaceful trade centers in many lands. In some of the lands of Islam these traders paid a tax of one slave in ten brought to the land to the ruling sultan.

FANTASIES AND OTHER SPECULATIVE THINKING

When writing was young, it was mysterious to most people since only a few knew how to read or write. Writing was tied to the sacred mysteries of the religion when taught to the acolytes, and each letter, pictograph, or hieroglyph could have a hidden, sacred meaning as well as a mundane sound and meaning. The complex systems of the Cabala and Numerology were tied to the Hebrew alphabet and the Arabic numbering system. So too the runes were tied to the religion and the culture of the people who used them.

Since each rune was a part of the runic alphabet, it represented a sound found in the language used. The runes, like the alphabet we use, could be more easily remembered by associating the rune with the sound it represents to a word starting with that sound, preferably one in which the rune's shape was found in the object it was logically associated with.

Additionally, sounds or tones are used by the adepts in many forms of meditation to induce changes in the state of mind and body. This has been seen in everything from the Gregorian chants of Christianity to the bells of Buddhist monks. This form of magic or meditation was also a possible use of the runes.

The fate of the runes as an alphabet and use in daily life can be understood with the quote of Han Solo. First, while the runes were in widespread throughout northern Europe, they were not taught to all members of the cultures which used them in depth. Most of the people who had knowledge of the runes were the very people most likely to be targeted for eradication to make the country more easily subjugated after being invaded. They were repetitively attacked though not totally subjugated by the Roman empire, then by the Christian legions of missionaries, and again by the Holy Roman Empire. In this latter period, from 800 to 1800 ce, the popes and bishops organized crusades not only to rescue the Holy Land from the Moslem, but also to eradicate Christian groups that did not bow their will to that of the pope as well as any pagan cultures.

Genocide has been widely practiced in man's history for religious and political conquests. This was being tried in Bosnia as late as 1994. Sometimes the invader wanted the land for their own, so the current inhabitants were slaughtered to the last adult, only virgin girls and very young children might be spared for slaves and concubines. As a race these people disappeared. In Bosnia, a concerted attempt to wipe out the race is the practice of rape and breeding of the minority out of existence when bullets don't work.

Sometimes the people were wanted on the land as slaves or "subjects" of the invaders. In these cases it was easier to just replace the political and religious leaders of the conquered tribes. Just kill the culture, not the people, and a few can rule many. This was successfully utilized by the communists in forming the U.S.S.R., and modern China. The invasion of the missionaries canceled the Viking nobles' and priests' use of runes by converting the nobles to Christianity and replacing the priests.

To put the last nails in the coffin of the runes, in the late Middle Ages, by the time of Charles V in the 1500s, it was heresy and a sure sign of witchcraft to be discovered with runes in one's possession. This carried a death penalty for any so caught. This can be seen in the example of the Druids which were killed off or forced to retreat by the invasion of Christianity. As an oral tradition, it was driven underground and eventually it was destroyed. Though Druid groups exist today, their lineage is often questioned by use of the "test of time" rule or questioning the authenticity of the documents the practice came from.

The history of the runes is more concrete since they are written, and the use of runes was widespread on many artifacts in daily use. When Christianity drove the runes' use underground because of their ties to the pagan deities, runes survived due to their links in the daily life of the people. Runes could still be found hidden in the art and artifacts of the people for many years, even after their religious significance was lost.

PERSONALLY SPEAKING

It is normally considered bad form for an author to include personal information in the subject matter of the book. However, since this is about the development of runic symbology in the psyche of people today, it is extremely subjective, not objective. In order for you to follow some of the intuitive leaps later, I will have to include personal information and background where relevant. There will be one other break with traditional format, I am including the bibliography of the references I used for this book, but I am not marking each reference with footnotes and other obstacles to readability.

I have been actively using and studying the runes since 1985, though I was introduced to runes over ten years earlier. I have been making rune products and giving runic readings for others since 1989.

I started meditating almost thirty years ago, and received instruction in several different forms from the near and far east as well as a couple of Occidental methods. In meditation, we learn that reality is subjective and filtered by our senses. We can develop abilities by training the mind. One of the abilities that is becoming more relevant in the last twenty years is the ability to take a holistic view of seemingly unrelated information, and by viewing it all as a system, to see relationships in the data.

I worked with astrology and numerology for a few years, and still consider them as valid tools for obtaining an overview of a person. I also tried the *I Ching* and various *Tarot* decks, but I found I cannot effectively utilize their symbology.

In school I studied psychology, philosophy, anthropology, comparative religions, and foreign languages while working on a degree in biology and chemistry. I utilized the analytical skills developed there as a computer systems engineer for over eleven years, combining analytical and intuitive thinking skills.

When I was first introduced to runes, they were given an unimpressive presentation. At the time, I was involved in study of the Nordic and Finnish legends and mythology, but did not get a firm connection between the runes and the myths. When I picked up Edred Thorsson's *Futhark* later, I finally made the connection. A few months later I was given the opportunity to have a runic reading done at a psychic fair.

As I studied the runes, the symbology connected for me. I made a set of flash cards to help study them, then I made a mind map of their relations and grouped the runes into families within the Elder Futhark. While working with the runes I had a flash of studying them from a rough board or plank. I transferred the idea to a small walnut table I had salvaged, and began to study from it. Later I carved a set of rune tiles for my own use from oak.

The more I used the runes, I began to see them in the light of my psychology courses as symbols with modern attributes described from an ancient perspective. They have been used in the religious heritage in northern Europe, yet they are still valid for modern man as the symbology they embody can be viewed as states of quantum physics, psychology, and chemistry.

While Edred Thorsson writes from the world view of the traditional Norse pantheon and use of the runes in magic, Ralph Blum writes from the point of using the runes in Christian divination. I write with the runes as symbols for the person, not necessarily tied to any one religion. Ancient, yet still full of meaning in the modern world, the runes are useful in the magical realm of the subconscious' dealing with reality. Like Ralph Blum, I do not feel that using the runes requires reversion to the worship of the Norse pantheon. The runes are open for use by anyone who connects with the symbology that the runes embody regardless of their religion. They are available to Christians, Pagans, Moslems, Jews, or anyone who wants them.

Now the stage has been set, and all the background scenes painted. Let's get down to showing the symbology of the runes in a form everyone can follow.

Chapter 3: THE INDIVIDUAL RUNES

The format to this section on the runes is arranged with a brief introduction of the rune giving the rune's name, phonetic, numeric, and symbolic correspondences in a short tabular heading. This is followed by the description of the rune where each of the symbolic representations are explained in varying detail. The short table is in the format of the flash cards I made to study the runes. The short summary information was on one side of the flashcard with the rune on the other. I will leave it to you to make your own flashcards if that is your wish.

The illustration at the beginning of the rune's discussion is in the form of a mandala. A mandala is a visual focus for meditation, normally formed with a repeating pattern or tunnel effect to draw the eye and the attention inward. In these mandalas, the rune overlays the diagram with meanings of the rune in symbol form repeating in the mandala. This is to keep the rune in the center of your attention with the symbolic meanings at the periphery of your mind.

Many of the runes can be interpreted with a spiritual, a mental, and a physical meaning, sometimes with a couple of meanings in the same plane of existence. The problem comes in determining which meaning was meant for any given position in a runic layout. Because of this multiplicity of meanings to the symbols, the discussions in this section deal with the rune in normal, upright position. If we were to attempt to cover all possible permutations of meaning in three planes of existence, with three possible orientations per plane, and all meanings for the symbols, this book would be a tome too heavy to lift and too boring to read, so some interpretation of position meaning is left for your subconscious to work out.

The pronunciation of the rune's title is in parentheses under the title. It is an English word where possible, and the stressed syllable is in all capital letters. In the pronunciation given by Edred Thorsson, ending "z"s are an "r" sound. I have spelled the title as phonetically as possible, where the "r" sounded better I replaced the ending "z" with an "r". In the case of HAEGEL - H, I am using the German name for the rune Edred Thorsson called Hagalaz. As R. I. Page pointed out, it is the beginning sound that was important for the purpose of writing, and in many cases, the name changed between the tribes, but the sound that started the name was always the same. In some cases the form was altered between the tribes, but in most instances the form was not changed until the sound it represented changed in the language.

RUNIC STATES

WYRD
(*WEIRD*)

0
DESTINY
SHON'JIR
DARKNESS
TAO, THE VOID
COLOR - BLACK
THE SHAMAN, THE WISE WOMAN
MONTH
MONDAY
THE MOON
SUBCONSCIOUS
WISDOM OF ODHIN

THE RUNE THAT WASN'T THERE -- OR WAS IT?

As I worked with the system of runes as described by Edred Thorsson, I found that there was an important part of life missing. There was a rune for the sun or daytime, but not one for the night or the moon. There were runes for a day and a year, but none for a month. The concept of nothing is important. How can you tell nothing is there, by its absence or presence? Think of the numbers, zero represents nothing, yet it is important for its use as a place holder, in fact it is absolutely essential to the development of quantum theories.

Why have a symbol for the sun in a language, but not one for the moon? There is no culture recorded that does not have a concept for the time period of a month or moon cycle or woman's cycle. Those cultures which use the moon cycle for the month have thirteen moons or months in the year.

So why is there no rune for the moon or a month? As I pondered this, I tried to work out what symbol should be used for such a concept using the rules for drawing the runes: straight lines for carving, preferably a shape that correlates to the meaning as seen in daily life. The moon changes shape from full to new moon with crescents between. The oldest Chinese pictograph for the sun is a simple square, then through use a line was drawn through the center of it to represent a day. Should I use a simple square or a crescent? A square could be mistaken for ING - ◊, and a crescent for KENAZ - く or JERA - ↯. Such a symbol would have been recorded all over, so why didn't Edred Thorsson or R. I. Page recognize it. The only answer to all of this is to represent nothing by a blank tile.

Those experts who acknowledge the blank rune, such as Ralph Blum, usually refer to it as destiny, unknowable fate. In his set of rune cards Ralph Blum has this represented by a moon on a cloudy night with six stars around it in almost a reverse of JERA - ↯.

If you want to find out which day belongs to which planet, look in any astrology book or a good unabridged dictionary. In most cases you will also find which deity is associated with the day, and so what each day is supposed to be the ruler of. Rather recently considering the antiquity of astrology, an astrologer compiled a list and reference of items to place them in the house they associate with, and to find which planets rule the items. He made the symbolic connections similar to those made in ancient alchemy to determine which of the four elements were in a particular item. The word Monday derives from the

Moon, and so the rune for Monday is the WYRD - , the blank rune. This is unfortunate in this case because the one rune is the moon, the night, the month, as well as Monday. Due to the planetary influence, this brings in the intuition, the family, and the mother.

Something still is not coming out yet, so let's look this over more closely. This rune represents the number zero, the void, the moon, the month, woman's cycles, the unknowable....

There it is. The missing pieces are hidden in close proximity, just turn over the taboo and you can see them, and possibly why this is the rune that doesn't exist for most people. In most patriarchal societies there is a taboo for dealing with a woman's period, that is an unclean time, a time of possible death, a time of separation. For most men this is a great and unknowable mystery. For many women, it was a thing accepted but not understood. The few who would understand this would be the shaman, the wise women of the tribe, and the old women who lived through the childbearing years and achieved menopause. That wise old woman who has passed the change and no longer can have children.

How many of you would dare to challenge a dark power that you were told basically from birth would kill you and enslave or kill your mind and use your body? Something invisible that you could not see or feel until it took your life force and it was too late? This is the strength of the taboo of the unknown. Even the gods were not exempt. Odhin nearly lost his life hanging on the Yew tree to obtain this knowledge, and he did lose an eye as the price to be paid to drink from the fountain of all knowledge.

It is no wonder that this is the rune of the blind eye that sees all, the darkest and most frightening nightmare, the thing that carries you off in the night, and the unknowable mystery. No wonder that this is the rune that does not exist for many. It is too fearful to contemplate for them.

Now suppose you are a woman to whom this knowledge is available if you should survive so long, or a man willing to risk his life and maybe more for the knowledge, maybe fearful of the possible consequences, but brave enough for a gamble, a shaman. What will you find in the darkness, the terror? As the Bene Gesserit said in Frank Herbert's *DUNE*; "Fear is the little death, the mind killer." The only way out is to walk through the pain, and the fear, until you walk out the other side.

As you walk through the darkness of fear you are confronted with the ultimate monster, yourself. You face your own subconscious fears and terrible aspects. Can you live with yourself, your actions, and the consequences of your actions? If you make it this far you find that the darkness is not just cold and inimical, it can also be the warm, comforting darkness of the womb. A place of love where you ready yourself for what is to come surrounded by your mother, a darkness you can return to for healing.

In Taoism, the void is a place of deepest meditation where the spirit can directly hear that still, quiet voice of the creator. But again, you must conquer your fears and throw yourself into a place of nothingness, risk the dissolution of your mind, your very identity. Sometimes drugs would be used to induce this state in training a shaman or wise woman. Those who could not stand this state would be rendered the ultimate horror, a mindless body, and an object lesson for the rest of the tribe.

C. J. Cherryh describes a game called SHON'JIR in a book of the same name. A warrior people, the players of Shon'jir sit in a circle clapping their hands. A pair of sword-knives are thrown to individuals in the circle at random by others in the circle. The concept of the game is to take your life, the weapons, in your hands and throw it into the Void of randomness in the circle, then to catch your life in your two hands when it is thrown back to you. That feeling is applicable to this rune and to the initiations into being a Shaman or Wise woman.

Could you lose your identity of being a man or a woman, being neither, yet having some of each, or being both a man and a woman at the same time? The deep dark fear of having no sexuality, no one to turn to and be accepted by as a brother or as a sister.

I call this rune the WYRD - , a destiny, usually fearful to contemplate, but only because of the pain of reaching it. To the old Viking culture, the WYRD - was similar to the eastern concept of Karma. It was the final effect of all of your actions in this lifetime. That is a return to the Void of creation, and the wisdom of Odhin. This is the rune of those initiated in the mysteries of life and death, the Shaman and the Wise Woman. It is the unconscious, the night, and the moon. It can be the fearful darkness of the Void, or the warm comforting darkness of the womb. It can be the game Shon'jir, accepting yourself and willfully throwing yourself into the circle of your destiny.

To look at the linkage of the blank rune to the others, it can be in a group related to time: day (DAGAZ - ᛞ) and night (WYRD -); day (DAGAZ - ᛞ), month (WYRD -), and year (JERA - ᛃ). If your tastes run to the Northern creation myths, it can be placed in the creation group with fire (KENAZ - ᚲ) and ice (ISA - ᛁ) as the void which existed before the two met and which surrounds us all. The void or chasm of the creation myth called "GINNUNGAGAP". As a day of the week, the languages of northern Europe relate the first day of the week to the moon, and therefore we relate Monday to the rune for the moon, WYRD -

This is a controversial rune when talking to those who study runes. Some deny the blank rune exists at all, that it does not fit in their neat system, it does not have a sound or part of the alphabet associated with it, nor can its presence be confirmed by finding it carved on an artifact. How can you see nothing, by its absence or presence?

This book is about the esoteric and mystical properties of the runes, and how they still fit into the psyche in the world of quantum physics. There are at least a dozen languages of the Germanic tribes that the runes were the alphabet for, so I use the languages I know when I use the runes. These being English, German, or French depending on my mood and task at hand.

One more comment on the meaning placed on the WYRD - . There are many books on the cultural taboos associated with menstruation, with the power of with blood, and so the danger to men posed by a woman in her period according to tribal beliefs. This is the same as any other power such as fire to them. It can cook your food, or burn down your house, caution is needed. It is for this reason a taboo is created, NOT because it is evil or unclean, just for the tribe's safety.

RUNIC STATES

FEHU (F)
(*FAY - hoo*)

1
CATTLE
MONEY
POSSESSIONS
HEALING ENERGY (NOURISHMENT)
PRIMAL EXPANSION MOTION
PRAYER OR BLESSING

THE BIG BANG

The concept expressed in the rune FEHU - ᚠ is traditionally twofold; that of possession or riches, and expansion. The name derives from the word for cattle, a form of mobile wealth for wandering tribes. Nomadic tribes either get stuck in a subsistence loop, unable to grow due to lack of resources, or they begin to expand linearly, conquering the sedentary agricultural communities. Just like a wildfire or a herd of cattle, they will consume the resources of an area and then be forced to move on to survive.

This principle is easy to see in the stadia or standing meditation position for the rune given by Edred Thorsson: a person standing with arms raised and outstretched. This position is the natural position assumed by a priest or priestess for prayers and blessings, both are out - sendings of power or desire or emotions. As a prayer FEHU - ᚠ sends out *SEE ME, HEAR ME, ANSWER ME IF YOU WILL, I AM HERE CALLING TO YOU.* This is the normal position for prayer, and can be found in almost all countries and cultures. The head bowed, wringing hands attitude for prayer is found mainly in one religious family tree. This more normal position can be seen in the shaman calling to the spirits or the mother of a starving child praying for food in Bosnia or Somalia. It is a call with an outpouring of energy.

What we have with FEHU - ᚠ is the more normal sending forth of a request to be answered. A strong sign of outgoing motion. While a symbol for mobile possessions and wealth, it specifically referred to the cow or cattle in its original context. Nowadays mobile wealth means an automobile, especially a Mercedes or Audi. It could even refer to a Winnebago type mobile home as well, in which retirees travel around the country.

Modern physics has a big bang theory for the creation of the universe. The universe started from a block of primal cosmic stuff, an explosion ripped it apart sending it out in all directions forming our expanding universe. In another couple of billion years the universe may slow and begin to contract, but for now it is still expanding. FEHU - ᚠ typifies this straight line outward expanding energy and motion.

Working this rune into your life brings constant motion, a driving force that does not let you rest in one place long like the itchy feet of the Gypsy and other modern nomads. Western society, especially the American culture, is filled with this restless energy from the Viking tribes which invaded the lands which settled North America. On an average, Americans move more than four times in their life, less rooted than many of the European cultures. Even some of the terms in our language shows this restlessness: upward mobility, fast track, and consistent advancement. With the poor corporate management of recent years, most people can only stay at one company for periods ranging from two to three years up to eight years. Gone are the twenty year careers with one company. Most companies are bought out and raided before they get to be twenty years old now.

The main thrust of this rune is outward expansion or flow. Prayer and blessings are both outward flows of energy from a sender to a receiver. Some forms of healing are also done in a similar manner. Either by prayer for the healing, or sending healing energy to cleanse or renew the sinking vitality of the receiver. Other forms of healing deal with growth and are covered in a later rune, BERKANO - ᛒ.

The down side to this rune is in it also means that as in a wildfire, to stay still is to die. Both the cattle movement and the wildfire is indicative of total consumption of available resources. The culture that brought the *Edda* and runes to Northern Europe was a conquering tribe that never settled down until it ran into a body of water it could not cross, the Atlantic. Even then, they could not stay in a place and be content to be herdsmen or farmers, they had to travel for gold and glory: to go a-Viking. This is also the primal power, the constant motion of the rune. A restless drive ever onward.

The groups we find FEHU - ᚠ linked to are those of the cycle of initiations as beckoning or prayer, that of money in the form of possessions, the runes of energy as primal expansion, and in the runes for healing as in the sending of cleansing energy.

There are three basic runes in the healing group, BERKANO - ᛒ which is growth and life, FEHU - ᚠ which is the energy that is poured out to the injury, and ANSUR - ᚠ, the incoming cosmic creator's energy we can use for healing. In the group dealing with money we find FEHU - ᚠ, the cattle and possessions, URUZ - ᚢ, the oxen that pulls the plow, and OTHALA - ᛟ, the prosperity of the homestead.

In chapter 5, there is a discussion of using the projective energy of FEHU - ᚠ in the rune wands. In this use, FEHU - ᚠ is a carrier wave of energy the runes that are placed beside it ride on. For example, a wand designed for healing would have BERKANO - ᛒ and ANSUR - ᚠ flanking FEHU - ᚠ at the tip of the wand. FEHU - ᚠ is the prayer and power for the wand's energy.

RUNIC STATES

BERKANO - B is placed on the outside of FEHU - F to add growth and healing to the energy of the wand. ANSUR - F adds an expectation of an answer to the prayer, and requests the spirits aid in the healing.

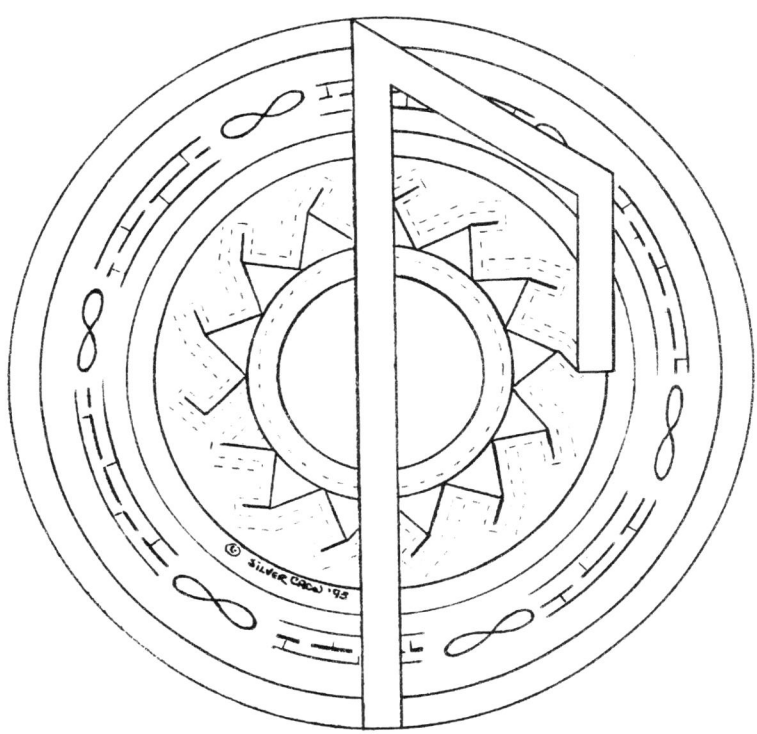

URUZ (U, V)
(*U - ruse*)

2
OXEN
PASSAGE
MATTER TO COME
PATTERN'S FORCE
WISDOM
OPPORTUNITY IN LOSS
STRENGTH

UNCOVERING YOUR STRENGTHS

Sometimes you need to be self-centered and a bit bullheaded in your dealings with difficulties. As a virtue this is known as perseverance. Through overcoming the difficulties, you can discover and develop your strengths and abilities. This is the main meaning of the rune URUZ - ᚢ, strength, with the bravery to persevere.

To find how we get that from the rune we need to look at the base of the rune, and what it meant to many of the early cultures. The base of URUZ - ᚢ is the definition of the ox, and everything else is derived from this.

In the *Edda*, the creation story tells of the fire and the ice at the ends of a vast chasm, the Ginnungagap. Where the fire met the ice, a vast steam cloud arose. From the drizzle of this mist a tremendous ox took form. This ox began to lick the ice and uncovered a giant, Ymir. Ymir fed on the milk of the ox, and grew even larger.

There are a myriad of cultures that worshiped or sacrificed the wild ox known as the Aurochs stretching from Persia, now Iran, to the Greek isles, to the cold realms of the Norse. As a sacrificial animal, we derive an opportunity or benefit from a loss. If the priests read the entrails, there was an opportunity to gain a foreknowledge of possible futures. The worship/sacrifice of the oxen comes from the time of the Goddess worshipping cultures, and the time when the God worshipping tribes conquered them. The ox is pivotal in many of the myths displacing the Goddess with the new deity, the God. This is very evident in the earliest stories of how Mithra came to power in the area that later came to be Persia.

Beside these two references, there is the use of oxen in daily life to consider. Instead of a tractor or truck, many wagons and heavy loads were pulled by oxen. The oxen were the strongest domesticated animal. After the advent of the plow, many a field was turned and planted with oxen. Many a person drank ox milk, ate ox, and probably wore ox hide shoes, at least when they wore shoes. Oxen, like horses, were well capable of finding their way home pulling a wagon as the driver slept. Wise? Perhaps, but they were also as likely to stop in a nice meadow and graze.

Shaped about like an ox, URUZ - ᚢ has two legs and a sloping back. This is also close to the shape of timbers or stone columns and cross pieces used to hold up the roof in a tunnel or passageway. These passages in many cases were, or could be associated with the sacred mysteries of a culture. Do you remember the Minotaur's Labyrinth? A bull headed humanoid in a maze of tunnels under the main temple in a Mediterranean capital to whom people were sacrificed. Mithra, the bull slaying god of the Persian empire and the Roman legions was also worshipped underground.

We have seen in the creation myth where the ox created its own pattern, and uncovered the matter that was to be the giant Ymir. In quantum physics, a photon of light shares the properties of a wave form (or pure energy), and particulate matter. In other words, there is a pattern defined by the Eigen value functions in which, if we were to view the photon as a particle or electron, we could see the greatest probability of finding the particle. This is the probability approaches the value of one or absolute certainty. This is the point in space where the wave form energy of the photon would turn to particulate matter known as an electron.

The mystics and magicians have a correlating law of magic. This is the law of visualization which states in order to create an object or event, it is necessary to create the pattern of it in existence by imagining it as already existing or having happened. This law is part of the reason that the oracles of antiquity were often thought of as self-fulfilling prophecies. The common sense of many cultures said to beware wizards since they rarely spoke the truth, but the future often proved them right.

Funny thing is the probability mathematics such as the Eigen value equations work in very much the same way, describing where the pattern is for the existence of the electron at some future point in time.

The sacrificial ox, the sacred passage, the force of a pattern, all of these deal with tying the individual to the universe and to other individuals. URUZ - ᚾ is where the mysteries of the mind work with the very force and act of creation, that of forming the pattern or blueprint that matter will later fill. This is the ultimate strength to uncover, how to work with your mind to plan the situation you wish to create.

In grouping URUZ - ᚾ into meaningful relations to see the pattern of the runes, I found it in four places. The first is in the group for the life cycle. The second is in the group for matter. The third is in the group for money. Finally, I placed it in the group for power.

The smallest group is that of matter with only two members: ISA - I, the primal matter; and URUZ - ⋂, the pattern that matter is formed around.

In the family group for money, there were three members placed, though traditionally, only FEHU - ᚠ is considered as being the rune of money as the cattle and possessions were traded as money. URUZ - ⋂ the ox, was also cattle, and traded as such, so by rights it belongs here without question. OTHALA - ᛉ is the farthest stretch to fit this category. Meanings of prosperity and freedom in this day and age mean having money, though excess possessions tend to tie one down, it is hard to be free to travel or seek pleasures if you are tied down working all the time, or are short of cash.

The grouping for the runes of power is much larger. In it we find ISA - I again, symbolizing inertia. FEHU - ᚠ is there as the primal expansion of the big bang, as is URUZ - ⋂ the pattern of the matter formed in the big bang. LAGUR - ᚱ is the life force of which science is just working on uncovering. KENAZ - ᛍ is the force of sub-atomic bonds found in quantum physics. In classical Newtonian physics we see ING - ◊ for potential energy, THURISAR - ᚦ for kinetic energy, and RAIDHO - ᚱ which represents mechanical energy. Two closely related runes in this group are HAEGEL - ᚺ, representing the wild elemental powers of the storm, and SOWHILO - ᛋ which stands in for electricity and atomic fusion of the sun.

RUNIC STATES

THURISAR (TH)
(*THUR - i - sar*)

3
THORN
MJOLLNIR
THURSDAY
GATEWAY
PROJECTED, APPLIED POWER
KINETIC ENERGY
VECTORS
NON-ACTION

THE THUNDER SPEAKS

The key to the symbology of THURISAR - ᚦ is the Norse God Thor. In all texts he is a symbol of strength, the defense of Asgaard with his mighty strength and terrible hammer, Mjollnir. His name is the root of the word thorn, as well as Thursday. Astrologically, Thursday is given to Jupiter, the wielder of the lightning bolts, and the ruler of business ventures. The symbol of Thor's hammer is an upside down capital T. THURISAR - ᚦ is close to the capital T on its side.

While Thor was not the strongest of the Norse pantheon, his son Magni held that honor, his immense strength was the key to the defense of Asgaard. His flashing hammer, Mjollnir, the lightning of the storms he ruled, always hit what he threw the hammer at, and always flew back to Thor's hand. This is the key to physic's concept of kinetic energy, the energy of objects in motion.

As the hammer was thrown, this rune is also the rune for projected energy and applied power. You could even say this is projected power or the broadcast power envisioned by Nikola Tesla in 1893 as well as the futurists and quantum physicists of today. This shape is also the arrows of vectors, the way forces are projected, measured, and inter-react.

I could stop here having covered the modern and ancient symbols for this rune. Yet there is more that can be said which is applicable to the other runes as well. So, let's take the detour and see what we can discover.

A thorn is a leaf that is specialized to protect the plant. Wrapping around itself it dries out gaining strength and rigidity. It is very similar to the stiff guard hairs in a porcupine's coat or your eyelashes. They both guard and protect, useful around an entrance or gateway.

A hedge of thorn bushes is used as a protective wall in many societies around the world. The thorns can also be used as a survival fishhook, a needle, or even a suture to close a wound. In the wild, a group of thorn bushes is known as a briar patch. Without some method for cutting through the obstructing vines, a person must wander on the paths under and through the entwined branches. All sense of direction is soon lost, resulting in the person wandering in circles until an exit is located, usually by accident.

This rune, THURISAR - ᚦ, has a caution seen here. It can caution you to not rush headlong into action, but think things through first. Thor was never renowned for thinking things through before swinging into action. He preferred a straight forward way of handling problems. Like the old Special Forces saying, *If at first you don't succeed, use a bigger hammer.* There was almost no problem Thor could not solve with his immense strength, his hammer, and a little assistance from his friends.

One of the key concepts in the preceding paragraph is how many friends Thor had. The popularity of Thor is seen in the many places named for him across northern Europe. There are mountains, hills, and towns named for him. According to some estimates, there are almost three times as many places named for Thor as there are named for Odhin. Everyone loved the boastful, drinking God of the Storms. The only enemies Thor had were the Frost Giants, including the ever troublesome Loki.

THURISAR - ᚦ also warns that you may find yourself wandering in circles, or stuck in repetitive cycles. This could be constantly getting into the same relations with various people as you get together, find the same faults, have the same fights, then break up, only to start all over again with someone else. You keep getting stuck in thorny relationships, in trying to protect yourself, you would rather destroy the relationship than lose your thorns.

Vectors are ways of seeing force and energy in physics represented by arrows, little thorns if you will, as such they have both a direction and a length or force component. Vectors hitting each other head on either may cancel each other out, augment the other if the polarity is right, or have the effect of combining and shooting off at an angle due to wave forms being slightly out of phase. The shape of THURISAR - ᚦ can be created by passing two lights through partial mirrors or polarizing plates which end up creating another beam off the incoming beam This is not like a mirror which just reflects the whole beam, but transmits some, and reflects some of the energy. In other words, a projected beam.

While Thor is the god of the thunderstorm, his rune is not associated as much with the lightning bolt as with his hammer. Yet it is his hammer that was his lightning bolt, the thunder was when it struck his target. SOWHILO - ᛋ, the sun, is the symbol for lightning instead due to its shape, and the shape of THURISAR - ᚦ. You may connect the two runes in this manner, yet the normal definitions are so different. One of the cases where the symbols diverge instead of converge, a meaning in common does not make the connection.

Most people do not make the connection of THURISAR - ᚦ to a group of protection runes as well. These are BERKANO - ᛒ for concealment, HAEGEL - ᚺ for banishment, EIHWAR - ᛇ for defense, ELHAR - ᛉ as a sanctuary, and OTHALA - ᛟ as a retreat to a safe house.

Almost everyone who thinks of grouping the runes will put this into a grouping for energy or force, and one for man made articles as a hammer, yet it is also a man-made article as a gateway, or more specifically the gate of thorns barring the way.

In working with a rune wand or bind rune we use THURISAR - ᚦ in two different ways. For protection we weave a ring of thorns around us, placing the ends of THURISAR - ᚦ together we can have a star or ring with any number of points from five on up, depending if we allow the various runes to overlap. For the rune wand we have a rune to project energy outward, similar to the way we use FEHU - ᚠ. If we start with a couple of energy runes at the top and bottom of THURISAR - ᚦ, THURISAR - ᚦ can take the energies being fed into it, and direct it out the end of the wand. On the way out the end of the wand we can place another rune as a filter so the energy is of the form we desire, that the wand will perform a specific function. An alternate way is to delete the filter, having THURISAR - ᚦ at the end with the desired runes feeding into THURISAR - ᚦ.

RUNIC STATES

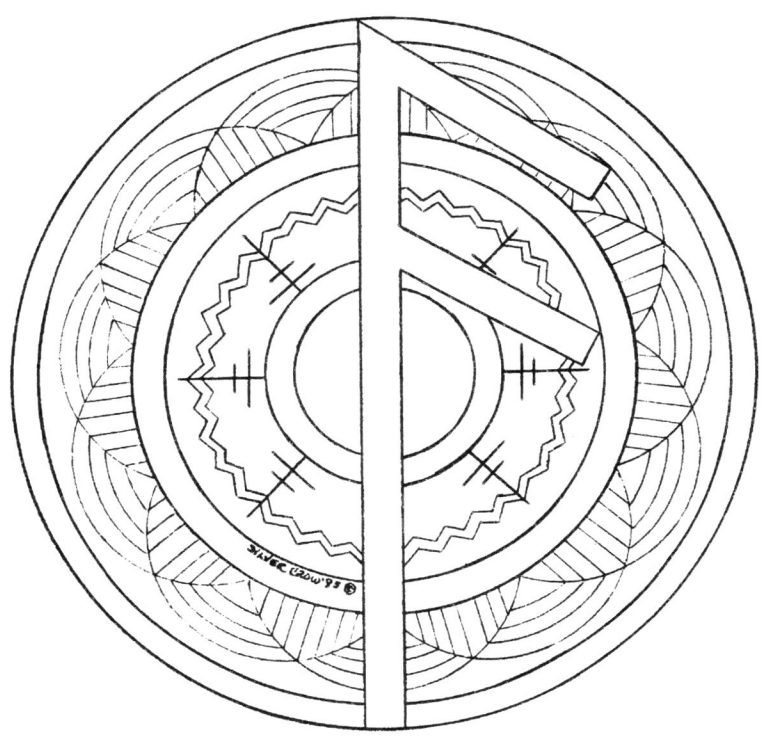

ANSUR (A)
(*ANS - er*)

4
MESSENGER
LOKI
ANIMATION
INSPIRATION
SPIRIT POWER AND KNOWLEDGE
SONG AND POETRY
COMMUNICATION
NEPTUNE

INTELLECT AND INSPIRATION OR DECEIT AND TRICKERY

In the discussion on PERTHO - ᛈ, we touch on the problem of inventiveness being desired yet shunned in the far past; how Loki was both a problem yet sometimes he helped to get the Gods out of the trouble he caused. ANSUR - ᚠ is the rune that deals directly with the God of chaos, Loki, the God of the quick wit and silver tongue.

ANSUR - ᚠ is a two edged sword of paradox. Inspiration, the power to deal with the spirits, and spiritual knowledge comes from Odhin, not Loki. However, in some cases Loki was used to deliver messages when Odhin was busy elsewhere. When dealing with this rune, who is the messenger delivering the gift? Is it Odhin himself, or Loki?

In the beginning of the association of Loki with the Gods and Goddesses of Asgaard, his quick wit and shape changing ability got Odhin and the other Gods out of some scrapes. So Odhin swore a pact of blood brotherhood, as seen in the rune MANNAZ - ᛗ, with Loki. Afterward they found out he was really of the giant blood, but with Odin's blood flowing in his veins, Loki could get across the Brifrost bridge and into Asgaard.

For a period of time, Loki was an exemplary model of a quick wit and inventive approach to solving problems. For this time, he was a trusted messenger for Odhin, passing inspiration and other gifts of the Gods to mankind. These other gifts were song, poetry, and spiritual knowledge which was a form of power. One of the other gifts he used was the animation of objects.

After a short while, some of the Gods recognized Loki's tendency to practical jokes and down right malicious tricks. His inventive approach to solving problems was also used in creating problems, tricks, and vengeful pranks. The only thing that saved him from being killed for his malicious tricks was being the blood brother of Odhin. This is one of the few pantheons that have a God of deceit and trickery and lies, one who gets away with killing another God through deception.

This rune ANSUR - ᚠ is both the answer of your prayers, and a gift of knowledge from Odhin, yet it could be a trick of Loki. There is an ancient Persian proverb that goes:

> He who knows not, and knows not that he knows not,
> is a fool; shun him.
>
> He who knows not, and knows that he knows not,
> is a child; teach him.
>
> He who knows, and knows not that he knows,
> is asleep; awaken him.
>
> He who knows, and knows that he knows,
> is wise; follow him.

BUT BE WARY!

The Germanic tribes were wary of all gifts from the Gods, because there was often a price to pay with them. The Gods normally did not get involved in the affairs of men, unless they could frustrate the schemes of the giants by doing so. With Odin's precognitive skills, the Gods helped men in order to help themselves at Ragnarok. To this end the Valkyrie searched the battlefields for the bravest and best fighters, to carry them to Valhalla to await Ragnarok. In order to ensure the best were taken to Valhalla, Odhin often gave victory to the weaker army, and constantly stirred up wars.

Another practice of Odin's was to set tests for heroes and other candidates for Valhalla. When you deal with Odhin or shamanism, there is a great potential for power, and a certainty that you will be placed in situations which will force you to grow up, develop yourself, and to move forward. After all, the entire motivation for Odhin is to protect Asgaard and to prepare for Ragnarok.

If you are going to gain the attention of Odhin, you must be prepared to be thrown into situations which will train, challenge and test you. When you work with shamanism and the runes together you will definitely draw the attention of Odhin. He is interested in heroes, not wimps. If you can not develop the moral character, skills, and courage he requires, there is little concern as to whether you pass or fail the test. The test will always be scrupulously fair, but very difficult, and failures can always be dangerous. Valhalla is not for the faint of heart, yet Odhin is never a trickster. He is always faithful to his word, look at the way he kept his oath to Loki, the ultimate troublemaker.

Today this rune, ANSUR - ᚠ, is communication in all of its myriad of electronic forms. When reversed, beware Loki's lies, yet when upright, it may hold the answer to your prayers as a gift from Odhin.

Astrologically, ANSUR - ᚠ relates to the planet Neptune, the planet of the arts and spiritual matters.

ANSUR - ᚠ is grouped with RAIDHO - ᚱ and TIWAR - ᛏ in matters of the spirit. Here, RAIDHO - ᚱ portrays spiritual development. TIWAR - ᛏ is the discipline of the spirit, while ANSUR - ᚠ is the knowledge and powers of the spirit matters. In creating the bind rune of the spirit called the Medicine Tree, I add EIHWAR - ᛇ to the rune group, even though it does not properly belong in a traditional definition sense. It was added because it is the tree of communication between the spiritual and physical planes. It is also the tree on which Odhin hung to discover the spiritual and magical runes. In a way, EIHWAR - ᛇ is the rune of spiritual quests.

ANSUR - ᚠ is also grouped with KENAZ - ᚲ and RAIDHO - ᚱ for matters of the arts. Here KENAZ - ᚲ is the creativity of the arts, RAIDHO - ᚱ stands for those arts which use rhythm and dance, while ANSUR - ᚠ stands for those arts of poetry and song.

Besides those two groups, ANSUR - ᚠ is in the group associated with the Gods and Goddesses, and with the life cycle group.

RUNIC STATES

RAIDHO (R)
(*RAID - o*)

5
WAGON
JOURNEY
DIVINE LAW AND ORDER
GOOD ADVICE/JUDGEMENT
SPIRITUAL DEVELOPMENT
RHYTHM AND DANCE
MECHANICAL ENERGY

AS THE WHEEL TURNS

In a circuitous way, wagons have wheels, wheels are circles, circles turn and thus are a form of cycle so let's go back to JERA - ᛃ. This would get us nowhere but back to the beginning so we need to discern where to stop the wheel's turn.

RAIDHO - ᚱ actually refers to a wagon or a journey in its original symbolism. In the far north, a wagon was often a sledge, or sled for short, with runners instead of wheels in the winter. This also ties it to the shaman's journey to the land of the dead where spiritual development and good advice or judgment was available. In this way the shaman has access to interpreting the divine laws, obtaining advice from the spirits, and in aiding the spiritual development of the tribe or the person the journey is undertaken for.

All methods of attaining the spirit lands involve a journey, though a shaman can walk, swim, or fly there, most of the time a device is imagined for use such as a canoe or a sled. Starting out in a sedate, controlled manner, the canoe or sled encounters a rapids or steep mountain slope which speeds up the journey and implicates a near death experience, though some shaman prefer to keep a sedate pace the entire way. The rhythm of drum beats, a rattle, or chants help the shaman attain the trance state necessary to perform this journey. Sometimes the shaman literally dances into an ecstatic trance from the rattle and drum and chants.

This sounds a lot like a rock and roll dance marathon doesn't it? In the final analysis, all music is based on a set of rules which make it possible to enter an altered, spiritual, state of mind. Many of the arts such as dance, drama, song, music, were created just to transport the actor into an altered state, to get across the message of a sacred play, while making all participants, including the audience, personal recipients of the spiritual growth or blessing of the art.

Where JERA - ᛃ corresponds to the non-physical cycles, RAIDHO - ᚱ is the symbol for physical cycles, in other words, wheels or gears, physical circular objects. This makes RAIDHO - ᚱ the symbol for many of our concepts relating to mechanical energy, a wound spring, clockwork gear mechanisms, pulleys and other circular assemblies to increase mechanical advantage.

In travel today, RAIDHO - ᚱ would represent our modern wagon, the automobile or truck. The journey in not necessary that of the spirit since we are much more mobile than the Germanic tribes were. Except for those who went a-Viking, most people would live their entire lives and never travel more than sixty miles from home. Now the journey can mean travel for any reason, from a vacation or business trip to moving all your possessions to accept a new job.

The shape of RAIDHO - R is close to a sled standing on end. When you lay RAIDHO - R on its back, the straight line becomes the runner of the sled. The simple expedient of adding wheels to the sides, the sled of the winter could become the wagon of summer.

In grouping RAIDHO - R with associated symbols, one is that of art containing KENAZ - < as artistic creation, ANSUR - F for the vocal arts such as song and poetry, and RAIDHO - R the more physical rhythm and dance.

In a group of spiritual symbolism, RAIDHO - R is the shaman's journey and spiritual development, TIWAR - ↑ is spiritual discipline, while ANSUR - F finishes the category being spiritual power and knowledge.

In the small group of travel, ELHAR - Y is by air, EHWAR - M is by foot, and RAIDHO - R is by car or train, while NAUDHIR - ↑ rounds out the list by representing travel by water or ship.

RUNIC STATES

KENAZ (K)
(*KEN - as*)

6
TORCH
OPENING
CONTROLLED FIRE
REGENERATION THROUGH
    DEATH/SACRIFICE
ARTISTS CREATION
HUMANITY
FRIDAY
PASSION/LUST (FREYA)
COLOR - RED
SUB-ATOMIC BONDS
BREATH
EXOTHERMIC REACTIONS

INTO THE FIRE

The rune KENAZ - < is a part of the Northern creation myths, fire. In the creation myths the fire (KENAZ - <) melts the ice (ISA - I) creating steam and water. It is from the steam and water that life came and everything else was made. KENAZ - < is the exothermic or heat producing chemical reactions. In daily life it can be the fire for cooking, the cauldron (pot) used for cooking, and the torch which gives light. Also represented is the fire of sacrifice and regeneration as in the Phoenix.

In a reading KENAZ - < can be the fires listed above or the passionate fires of humanity and the creative acts of the artist. It counsels action with appropriate controls. When you look at the shape of the rune, it opens from left to right and could be an opening or opportunity forming.

In KENAZ - < we find Friday, devoted to the planet Venus, named for the Norse Goddess of love and fortunetelling, Freya. The planetary influence is that of the hedonistic tendencies, love of person and love of property or of acquisitions. The rune KENAZ - < seems out of place at first until you look at the heat of passion in love, and the method of fortunetelling used by Freya was that of the fire in a brazier. This is the method she taught to Odhin for contacting the dead, and the method used by Nostradamus, and many of the Greek and Roman oracles in divination.

A note aside may be in order here. There are as many dictionaries who show the derivation of the word Friday being associated with Frigg, the wife of Odhin, the Goddess of hearth and homemaking or marriage as those who associate it with Freya. While this would still fit with KENAZ - <, it ignores all the cultures where Friday is associated with Venus, passion and love, not so much the matron of the hearth as the concubine or mistress of passion's flame.

Lets look at this a bit more. What was fire used for in the period the runes were used? It was for cooking and heating the home, for burning the fields in the spring, cremating the warrior in some instances, forging the metal implements, a source of light, sacrifices, and a deadly weapon or disaster when out of control. There are two more instances of a form of fire from other areas. The Kalevala of the Finns spoke of the fire from the sword of the creator which came to man in a time of darkness, and the Indian continent had a fire of life associated with the Prana, the breath of life. I believe these hidden fires are in reference to the invisible radiations of atomic and sub-atomic nature.

What does contemporary science think of fire? Energy in all wavelengths released by the combustion of material. In other words energy is released from the breaking of atomic bonds which includes atomic energy. Normally, the fire is a self-feeding loop: the heat causes a change of state to a gas which ignites, combining with oxygen and releasing more heat. Strangely enough, energy can be released in both the breaking of the bonds, and in the forming of new bonds of greater strength. Atomically, when an atom loses a bond, the excess energy is radiated out with both particle and wave form attributes, sometimes loosing an electron in the process.

So where does the form of this rune come from? Ralph Blum suggests the chance crossing of a pair of sticks in flame, Edred Thorsson would make it seem that it is from the taper of a torch. Since fire is so amorphous, there is no simple easy way to show a fire. Ask a child to draw a fire: you may get the flame of a candle or the flames shooting out of a burning building. The tip of the flame is like a downward opening KENAZ - < Rune.

I am more inclined to think of the angle the steel needs to strike the flint to make a fire, or the notch you cut into a fire board to make a fire with bow and drill as being the beginning of this rune. For those of you who find these fire making attributes too untenable, you need only look for the form of KENAZ - < in the definition of the passionate fires of Freya and consider her opening in passion to find the shape of KENAZ - <.

The rune KENAZ - < is linked to five groups. The first is in the Northern creation myths with ice (ISA - I) and the void (WYRD -) or Ginnungagap, the chasm which contained it all. In another it joins the sun (SOWHILO - ᛋ) to show regeneration, just as the fields were burned before planting. It also links to the energy runes: inertia (ISA - I), kinetic (THURISAR - ᚦ), fate (NAUDHIR - ᚾ), life (LAGUR - ᛚ), fire (KENAZ - <), potential (ING - ◊), primal or mental (FEHU - ᚠ), and that of a pattern (URUZ - ᚢ). KENAZ - < is the creation rune for the artistic group with rhythm and dance (RAIDHO - ᚱ), and ANSUR - ᚨ for songs and poetry. It also represents the feminine passions and fertility in the guise of the goddess Freya where it matches JERA - ᛃ which stands for the masculine passions and fertility of Freya's brother Freyr.

RUNIC STATES

GEBO (G)
(*GAY - bow*)

7
GIFT
WEDDING
HOSPITALITY
TWO/MANY IN ONE
ECSTASY
PSYCHIC UNION
PLATONIC LOVE (PARTNERSHIP)

THE SUM OF THE HEART

There is an old poem that ends "The sum of the heart is done, to prove that one and one makes one." This is the heart of the lesson of GEBO - X. The shape of GEBO - X is two sticks crossed, the old sign for hugs that your grandmother put on letters, an X.

GEBO - X is also the psychic union and platonic love that is needed for a partnership in a business. While EHWAR - M is the marriage, GEBO - X is the wedding, the actual joining of two peoples. This rune is the political side of the wedding, a peaceful joining of two houses or businesses, not the marriage which is the wedding bed and the children which would fall under EHWAR - M.

This is the divine gift, the wedding gift, the gift of hospitality to strangers...the gift of civilization. When you get right down to the bottom of the matter, GEBO - X is the rune of getting along with people, of caring for someone else and treating them in an ethical manner. It is having empathy for them, and thus being able to work with them.

The culture of the Germanic tribes was tied together with the giving of gifts. Kings paid for loyal services with gifts of gold, land, titles, etc. Families and countries were also united with the gift of the dowry that accompanied the bride to the wedding. The stature of a man in the community was not determined as much by the amount of gold or land he owned, but by his generosity. With every gift given, stature increased, and political influence in the community increased with stature.

In a quantum sense, there is no real meaning to this rune, since Einstein never completed the unified field theory to find where gravity fits with the electromagnetic spectrum. GEBO - X is the ultimate joiner, so GEBO - X would be appropriate for this theory of unification that is not finished.

Most of the uses for GEBO - X is in creating bind runes as the center that joins four runes together. The straight line that forms the back of most runes is placed on one of the radial lines of GEBO - X. The resulting word or group of symbols is joined in the union formed by GEBO - X.

Everything joined with GEBO - X is on the platonic or psychic level, even the ecstasy is that of the cuddle or joy of working well together, not sexual ecstasy.

RUNIC STATES

WUNJO (W)
(*WOON* - yo)

8
JOY
HOPE
HARMONIC PRINCIPLE
NEW ENERGY
CLAN BANNER
FELLOWSHIP
HARMONIOUS BINDING
SYMPATHETIC ATTRACTION

THE BANNER OF THE CLAN

The second rune in the grouping of mankind is that of the clan banner, WUNJO - ᚹ. In the grouping for humanity WUNJO - ᚹ is joined by mankind (MANNAZ - ᛗ), and the clan house (OTHALA - ᛟ). The reason we place it second is that in moving from the smaller to the greater, MANNAZ - ᛗ is the ego, and blood brothers or close blood kin. This is a factor of one or three to about a dozen. WUNJO - ᚹ is the clan banner, and all who gather under it. Taking in those who live in a village, or just aunts, uncles, cousins, as well as the close kin of siblings and parents, the number is easily twenty or more. In OTHALA - ᛟ, the clan house and ancestral lands, this number grows even more to include in-laws and ancestors of note.

There is never a lot written about this rune, it seems to be the most straight forward of all the runes. The shape is that of a pennant on a staff, or the banner that flew over the clan. As the banner of the clan it denotes the harmony of the clan, joy of the family, and fellowship. Thus it is the rune for any collection of people of a like mind, or those who are gathering and united for a purpose.

In the realm of physics WUNJO - ᚹ rules the harmonic principle and the world of sound. When sound waves are in harmony, they reinforce and build on each other. If the harmony is just right, a standing wave is formed, seeming to freeze the motion of the wave.

It can stand for the new energy of a leaf shooting forth from the ground in the spring (the banner of a plant). It also is the joy or transcendent feeling of happiness and well being of a beautiful day in spring, or when working in a harmonious group.

Since it represents the fellowship of the group, this rune is also that of sympathetic attraction, and useful in making a bind rune. It has the ability to bring out the cooperation in the runes selected for the bind rune, focusing the energies to the task at hand, the reason for the bind rune. As a rune for creating harmony or binding things together there is a group with just members, WUNJO - ᚹ and GEBO - X, the first is many acting as one, and the second is where two become one.

The last group for WUNJO - ᚹ is that of the articles that mankind created. It can represent a flag or a banner and so is allied to the other mancrafted articles: the hammer (THURISAR - ᚦ), the wheel (SOWHILO - ᛋ), the house (OTHALA - ᚨ), the dice cup (PERTHO - ᚦ), the wagon (RAIDHO - ᚱ), the ship (NAUDHIR - ᚾ), and the torch (KENAZ - ᚲ).

RUNIC STATES

HAEGEL (H)
(*HAY - gel*)

9
HAIL
DISRUPTION
PRIMAL SEED
RUNE MOTHER
PROTECTION AND BANISHMENT
RADICAL DISCONTINUITY
ELEMENTAL POWER

SHIPWRECKED IN THE STORM

The term used in this book a-Viking may seem strange to many, and to others it raises their hackles. In fact, the word Viking is like the word Explorer, both are terms for the people who performed an activity, where the name is the same as the activity. Explorers explored while Vikings vikinged, but that gets us into trouble when you say vikinging. The term Viking originally did not mean the people, but the reason for the journey the people were on. Going a-Viking was a type of trading voyage, going for fame and riches, with a little piracy thrown in. The object was to see new lands, trade, make a bit of a profit, and like many traders of the time, protecting yourself and your goods from being stolen.

When the Viking set sail there were two main threats to the goods in the ship; storm and shipwreckers. Of course when they ventured into the Mediterranean, there were the pirates and the occasional navy to worry about, but the main two hazards were the storm and the shipwrecker who would lure ships onto unknown shoals.

Originally HAEGEL - H meant the hail of the storm and the elemental powers of the fierce storms. This power caused many a shipwreck by itself. Normal hail hurts and stings when it hits, but once in a while truly monstrous storms hit, those with golf ball or baseball sized hail. These will kill unprotected people, even if the lightning misses them.

The shape for HAEGEL - H is either that of the capital H with a sloping cross bar, or something similar to an asterisk, (*), except having eight points. It is said in Nordic mythology that this eight pointed form is the older form from which all the other runes came, just like the block of ice was the primal matter from which everything came in the creation myth in the *Edda*. In its way, that made it a chip off the mother block, or a primal seed from which things can grow. In fact, many of the other runes can be seen buried in this primal shape, but not all. This alternate shape of an eight spoked wheel without a rim is known in other cultures as a symbol of Chaos, which can be considered the disruption of HAEGEL - H.

When you work from the viewpoint that the fates never send out good luck like the ancient Northern cultures did, anything from them is bad luck sent to stop you from getting too cocky. So when a good voyage is getting close to home and a storm comes up, it is probably the fates trying to knock you down. So the hail and disruption it caused became feared as sending of the fates to rob you of your hard earned successes.

Of course there is the other side of the story. For the fishing folk at the edge of the sea, a storm could be hard, but not always as devastating as to those on the sea. After a storm, everyone would head down to the beach and see what the storm washed up. It could be a ship, or cargo from a ship, but most often it was food for the hungry in the fish caught on the beach dead or in tidal pools. It could also be seaweed for medicine and soups, or sea shells to make combs and jewelry from. A few men were unscrupulous enough to put out lanterns to draw the ships not into safe port, but onto the shoals in the storms. If they would just kill the survivors, the ship's cargo was theirs. These were the shipwreckers, drawing bounty from the storm.

Like many of the medicines that our western science loves, a little will cure you, more will kill you, so HAEGEL - H also was used as a protective amulet like a modern vaccination. If the fates could send HAEGEL - H to everything, and if you then used HAEGEL - H in an amulet, maybe the protective amulet would then keep some of the misfortunes away. After all, similar poles on a magnet repel, not attract. It was worth a try to beat the fates at their own game, to tone down the major misfortunes, and avert the minor ones altogether.

This leaves the two symbols for the psyche and quantum aspects to be covered. A discontinuity is a break or flaw in an established pattern while a radical discontinuity is a dramatic break in the pattern. If you look at the sun or a star through a spectroscope, you will see black bands which indicates elements that are missing, or more precisely, you will see only those bands of excitation for the elements that are present. A disruption is close to the same, something that breaks the patterns in your life.

One of the major disruptions in your life as an adult is being fired when a plant shuts down or is scaled back because some corporate raider bought it and is skimming everything he can into his pockets. An accident around the home is another. Most of the small disruptions are attempts by your subconscious or superconscious to wake you up and to get you to think about what is going on. It may be something more major, a radical discontinuity, like loss of a limb, or winning a million dollars in the lottery. It does not have to be bad, or totally unplanned for, but sometimes life requires a kick of major proportions to get out of a rut, to get a life cycle moving again.

That is the first spot we will find HAEGEL - H, in the group of runes for the cycles of life. The full meanings to this group is found in the next chapter on groupings, but basically covers the three stages found in a cycle in life.

LIFE CYCLE

HAEGEL - H	DISRUPTION
KENAZ - <	OPENING
NAUDHIR - ↑	NEED
FEHU - F	PRAYER
ING - ◊	GESTATION
URUZ - ᑎ	PATTERN TO COME
PERTHO - ᒷ	ÓRLOG
ANSUR - F	INSPIRATION
OTHALA - ᛉ	SEPARATION
EHWAR - M	TRANSITION
RAIDHO - R	JOURNEY
BERKANO - B	GROWTH
DAGAZ - M	BREAKTHROUGH

The only other group in which we normally find HAEGEL - H is that for forms of water: ISA - I, ice, HAEGEL - H, hail, and LAGUR - ſ, flowing water. HAEGEL - H is also in the family of protective runes, but most people do not trust the power of HAEGEL - H in defense since it is so chaotic and may burn down the house it was supposed to warm.

RUNIC STATES

NAUDHIR (N)
(*NOW - deer*)

10
FATE'S POWER
NEED
COMPULSION
CONSTRAINT
RESISTANCE
SHIP'S MAST
WILL DIRECTED ACTION
CAUSE/EFFECT

WHEN THE NEED IS GREAT

There are many often quoted rules or laws of magic in esoteric literature. Most are from esoteric Christian teachings, and show the bias of early Christian doctrine. Some examples are that you must abstain from sex to do magic, and if you use your powers for yourself you will lose them.

In contrast to the first bias is the Tantric form of Yoga which is devoted to harnessing the energy of sex to accomplish magic. As for the other example, there are thousands of people who will argue both ways, especially since the Christian world view is so prevalent. In this instance it is a case of what you believe is true for you. If you believe you will lose all use of your gifts, then so you shall.

The world view and cosmology of the Germanic tribes were quite advanced in their realization of how magic will or won't work for you. They should have been since most of the world was magic, not science or technology. NAUDHIR - ↑ played an important part in their views, indeed it is just as important now. For in their own way, these tribes of a thousand years ago knew much of the laws behind reality, those of the subconscious and the mind, the Örlog of the rune PERTHO - ⌐.

The fates controlled the destiny of men and the Gods. NAUDHIR - ↑ was the base of their power to do so. This was a great need to fill the pattern of the worlds that they saw. The fates were totally knowledgeable about the cause and effect of modern science, and could apply the correct minimal nudge to cause what they saw to come to pass. They used HAEGEL - H, a sending of disruption, to knock men and Gods out of their complacent and comfortable habits, forcing them to move and to change.

The keys to bringing the laws behind reality to play, to establish a fortuitous synchronicity to come in to being are imagination, need, and faith. If you do not have the faith that what you do will work, you send out negative vibrations for each positive act you wish to create. These will cancel each other out. A great need symbolized by NAUDHIR - ↑ will help provide the faith for your attempt, or at least cancel any negatives you may be feeling.

This is not just a little need or a want, but a need you feel with the whole of your being. The imagination sets forth the image or pattern, URUZ - ∩, of what you desire to occur. NAUDHIR - ↑ provides the impetus to fill the pattern of your desire.

After you have sent out this great need, be it for yourself or for others, the Örlog forces represented by PERTHO - C begin to set the stage for the appearance of your wish. This does not mean you do nothing else, for you have only set a causal force into play. As your magical will, SOWHILO - ϟ, keeps working on the problem of actualizing your desire, you will find circumstances arising which require your will directed actions (NAUDHIR - ᚾ) in normal reality. These can be constraints (NAUDHIR - ᚾ) to perform or refrain from performing planned acts. This then sets up the physical cause and effect to bring your mental cause and effect into your reality.

It is important to feel this immense need in order to overcome the resistance (NAUDHIR - ᚾ) or inertia of reality to change. To give it that HAEGEL - H kick out of the rut you and it are in. Think of any large project you have worked on. Unless the need is great, you can only chip away at getting the results you want. It takes so long and so many repetitions to achieve any sort of result. When the need is great, suddenly backers appear from everywhere to help with either moral or actual physical assistance. That is the Örlog in PERTHO - C moving behind the scenes to bring the pattern you created into physical reality.

The Germanic tribes held the basis in NAUDHIR - ᚾ for cause and effect in their culture which did not spread to the rest of the European continent until the renaissance four hundred years later. Some of this was negated by the dogma of the Christian church when it arrived a short two hundred years later, but a foundation that critical thought could rest on was already in place.

The shape of NAUDHIR - ᚾ is that of the spar of a ship angled across the mast before the sail is set on it, or a pivot bar to lock a door. The best match to the meaning is that of the spar for the sail. The sail catches the wind, providing resistance which allows the ship to move forward. Without resistance of the sail to the wind, and the keel to the water, there can be no movement, for like cause and effect, movement requires a resistance or thrust of mass in the direction opposite of the movement. When we walk we push against the ground, when we swim we push against the water, and when an airplane flies it pushes air back to move forward.

The grouping for the Germanic fates includes three runes. There is NAUDHIR - ᚾ which is the power that the fates use to achieve their ends. PERTHO - C is the Örlog, the rules and laws by which the power symbolized by NAUDHIR - ᚾ works. Finally there is the WYRD -   , or the destiny they see and tie man and the Gods to.

One other group that NAUDHIR - ✣ shows up in is the life cycle group. As described above, in this group NAUDHIR - ✣ is the great need that kicks you between the eyes and wakes you up to the dissatisfaction with your current situation event though the kick is delivered from the foot of HAEGEL - H.

The last group that NAUDHIR - ✣ shows up in is that for travel. NAUDHIR - ✣ is the mast and spar of a ship, ELHAR - Y an airplane, RAIDHO - R a car or train, and EHWAR - M is travel by foot, horse, or motorcycle.

RUNIC STATES

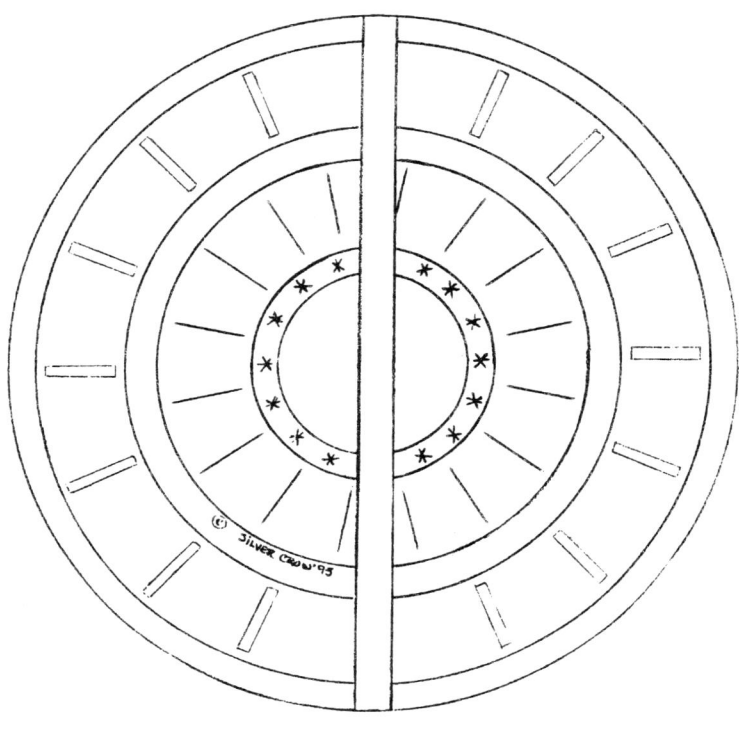

I

ISA (I)
(I - ssa)

11
ICE
COLD
PRIMAL MATTER
STILLNESS
IDENTITY
PATIENCE
COLOR - WHITE
ENDOTHERMIC REACTIONS/COLD
PLUTO
INERTIA

THE STILLNESS OF ICE

The rune ISA - I is a part of the Northern creation myths, ice. In many of the northern countries, ice and it's smaller counterpart, snow, are vital to life. In the coldness of winter, life sustaining water becomes ice. The flowing stream of water gets a cold, still covering of ice. The shape of ISA - I is that of an icicle, a single straight line.

The northern countries mythology also shows that ice is to be feared, the coldness of winter is the time of the Ice Giants, the almost eternal nemesis of the Gods and of man. It is these Ice Giants that are the incarnation of evil in the mythology of the North. All that is feared is a product of the Giants or their cousins or their offspring. Though there are a few of the giants and half breed offspring that rose above their evil nature, they often returned to their base nature. The best example is the ultimate traitor and cunning god of chaos, Loki.

The concept of ISA - I has the same power as absolute zero and entropy in physics. It is the matter from which everything comes into being, the potential of energy and matter, the cosmic egg of the big bang theory, the block of ice from which all was created.

In a reading, ISA - I counsels inaction or the cultivation of patience. On the mental level it represents the identity of the individual, that stable and mainly unchanging part that says *I AM ME!* It can also signify the force of inertia and endothermic or cold producing chemical reactions. It can herald a changed condition as when soft, yielding water becomes hard and sharp ice. It also represents the color white.

Astrologically Pluto is the planet of introspection, the subconscious, and psychic matters. This is a very heavy planet astrologically, while astronomically it is slow moving and stable, therefore I placed it with the rune ISA - I. Just as the glacier made of ice is slow to change and move so are matters of the personality unless there is a momentous cataclysm to precipitate the changes.

The rune ISA - I is linked in three rune groups. The first is in the Northern creation myths with fire (KENAZ - <) and sometimes the void (WYRD -). In another linkage, matter (ISA - I) joins one more, the pattern of the matter (URUZ - h). The largest group it links to is that of energy runes. These are inertia (ISA - I), kinetic (THURISAR - ▶), fate (NAUDHIR - ✦), life (LAGUR - ↑), fire

(KENAZ - <), potential (ING - ◊), primal or mental (FEHU - F), and that of a pattern (URUZ - n).

With ISA - I, we have covered the first of the groupings of runes, those relating to the creation myth. So let's take a look at beginnings. Ralph Blum in his Christian world view has the beginning coming from divine inspiration. However, the normal ordering of the runes begins with FEHU - F which could be a prayer or blessing, and ANSUR - F which could be divine inspiration comes four places down as an answer to the prayer.

The creation myth whose runes we just finished is more of a quantum look at life with space or a void, energy, and matter coming together. The only item missing from the normal quantum physics view of the beginning of the universe is a pattern. You have a big bang, but where is there a set of laws by which the energy and matter come together in space?

As an example of how the runes could be used in teaching a creation myth similar to that proposed by the Germanic tribes, let us examine a myth using the runes to show what is being said. In the beginning was the void (WYRD -), a giant chasm with fire (KENAZ - <) at one end, and ice (ISA - I) at the other. A primal need (NAUDHIR - ↑) following the Örlog laws (PERTHO - C) and the pattern (URUZ - n) created a giant ox from the steam where the fire met the ice. This ox (URUZ - n) licked at a block of primal ice (HAEGEL - H), and formed the earth father (ING - ◊) and mother (BERKANO - ß), not necessarily in that order. These then created the sun (SOWHILO - ϟ) so that there may be day (DAGAZ - M) and that the water (LAGUR - r) of the earth could bring forth life (ELHAR - Y). After the season of growth (JERA - ϫ), the grains (FEHU - F) could be harvested by mankind (MANNAZ - M) and the Gods (various runes) which the union (GEBO - X) of ING - ◊ and BERKANO - ß brought about. The world axis (EIHWAR - ↕) connects the realm of the gods with that of man, and allows both the divine inspiration (ANSUR - F) and divine laws (RAIDHO - R) to be communicated to mankind. When mankind follows this guidance and acts (THURISAR - þ) upon it, spiritual discipline (TIWAR - ↑) and harmony (EHWAR - M) results in joy (WUNJO - r) and the establishment of clans with their lands and villages (OTHALA - ⍟).

Please note that this myth diverges from that given in the *Edda* where Ymir, a Giant, was the first uncovered from the block of ice. Suckling on the teats of the ox, he grew so large he almost filled Ginnungagap. The ox continued to lick, and uncovered next the Gods of Asgaard, Odhin and three brothers, then the first man and woman of Midgaard. Midgaard, or the earth was formed from the skull of Ymir after the Gods slew him.

RUNIC STATES

JERA (J, Y)
(YAR - a)

12
YEAR
HARVEST
CYCLE
KARMA
FERTILITY (FREYR)

BECAUSE YOU DESERVE IT!

JERA - ᛃ is the rune of just desserts. No matter how you say it, everyone recognizes some form of the folk saying *As you sow, so you reap.* Somewhere, sometime, you will get what is coming to you is stated in *What goes around, comes around.* Even more we speak of peoples past will catching up with them. You will be treated as you have treated others. The old karma will sneak up on you.

The literal translation of JERA - ᛃ is year. In German it is spelled a bit differently, but pronounced the same. The only question is did the Germanic tribes celebrate a solar or lunar year? In the folk tales you hear of magical servitude being a year and a day. The Celtic myths are full of this, as are some of the Norse and Germanic area stories. This points to a lunar year. Thirteen moons is 364 days. The extra day is known as the day between the years, added to make the lunar year equal the 365 days of the solar year. These stories are not in the *Edda*, but other folk tales.

So far I gave two definitions but not the connection. In this case the connection is key as to what JERA - ᛃ is. Agrarian people lived by the harvest. If the harvest was small, people starved, if they could not supplement the harvest with hunting, people died. Without the science bred seeds of today, it was not unusual for only one seed in ten or one seed in twenty to germinate. Plant all the kernels on an ear of corn and you may get five or ten stalks of corn. In that case, it would take at least ten or twenty ears to hope for a small field of corn to feed a family for part of a winter. Even then, they would have to set aside at least the same number of ears for planting the next year.

Obviously fertility of the field, the crops, and the herd was vital to survival. Also vital was that everything lived until harvest, and provided seed for next year in addition to what would be eaten in the winter.

These people recognized the cycles of nature, both short term, yearly cycles, and cycles in a lifetime. In being the symbol of the cycle this rune is especially pertinent to life today. Everyone is talking of recycling, an aspect of the cycle and thus of JERA - ᛃ, but fewer realize the scope of the cycle concept in science. The cycle started to be recognized in the natural sciences talking about evaporation and precipitation in the water cycle. It was picked up by the life sciences in the food chain shown as a cycle, and eventually founded the ecological disciplines which work on the theories of cycles and systems. Eventually even the physical sciences began looking at systems and energy cycles. Instead of just an expanding universe theory, we now have an expanding/contracting universe theory in which the currently expanding universe will begin to contract in a few billion years, then the cycle will start all over again.

In the discussion of ING - ◊, I touch on the sacrificial regicide that some cultures practiced in conjunction with the harvest, and how it could be a key to the shape of JERA - ◊. One of the other ceremonial practices could be used to get the shape of JERA - ◊. In this one the shaman or other religious leaders would ceremonially extinguish the hearth fire of the tribe, then make a new fire which would be kept burning for the next year. So by this ceremony we have JERA - ◊ being formed by two KENAZ - < runes facing each other, separated and offset by a small space.

Both of these ceremonies are designed to promote new life and fertility for the tribe. In the first, the old and supposedly used up male leader was replaced, in the second only the sacred fire was replaced. For those tribes worshiping the pantheon of the *Edda*, this fertility was symbolized and embodied in the God, Freyr, and his sister the Goddess Freya.

With some Pagan and Heathen traditions, the time of the fall harvest is considered the New Year. With others, it is the winter solstice on the 21st of December. One dictionary said the Chinese New Year is figured as the first full moon after the winter solstice. One interesting point is part of the New Year's celebration is to pay off all debts possible to start the New Year with a clear slate. It is interesting in the analogy of clearing debts, clearing karma, and JERA - ◊.

A side trip with some interesting scenery exists in JERA - ◊. The Norse pantheon of the Germanic tribes was a typical male dominated collection similar to the Judeo/Christian/Moslem history in several aspects. The first aspect is the religion is of an aggressive group of tribes with an impressive list of wins on the battle field. These are not the type of people to sacrifice the king at the end of the year. The queen or a concubine would be much more expendable. Therefore a logical connection could be made for their use of the solar New Year at the winter solstice than the autumnal equinox of Goddess worshipping and male sacrificing cultures. The new day and new year does not start at dusk or dawn, but rather in the deepest and darkest middle of the night when the sun begins it's return.

By this time, you may have noticed a vacillation between Goddess and God oriented descriptions of the runes. In no rune is this more poignant that in the offset mirror image of JERA - ᛃ. This is the only rune which is divided in two separate parts like humanity is divided into male and female.

Much of the early history of mankind has evidence of Goddess worshipping tribes. In all cases, these were later overrun by God worshipping tribes or were later bludgeoned into accepting Christianity by missionaries, or the military might of Christian nations. Historically, there was a third form of religion, actually of spiritualism which worked with both God and Goddess worshipping people. This third way was Shamanism; Male or female, the shaman was the medium between the spirit world and the realm of humanity. Until the monotheistic priests started to usurp this function, dealing with the spirits was separate from the religion of the tribe.

As my studies commenced, I found more and more indications that Odhin, the supreme commander of the *Edda's* pantheon was by the definition and his actions, a shaman. Thus the God which gave us the runes was a gender spanning shaman. This is not the only gender crossing God, Loki, but gender spanning. Loki was the only one capable of actually becoming a functional female who became pregnant and bore young as a female, and sired young on a female. Odhin, as a shaman, visited the lands of the dead, and utilized a feminine form of divination normally shunned by males.

Here we again look at the shape of JERA - ᛃ. It is the mirror image of two parts facing across a gap that cannot be crossed, yet two complimentary parts of a whole, one slightly superior in elevation than the other. In the Germanic tribes, the woman was not chattel of the man, only slightly less in social stature than the man. The wife held the keys to the stead in the Germanic tribes, the de facto ruler of the home and hearth. A woman could divorce her husband and reclaim her dowry in her own right. There is even a case of a woman divorcing her husband because the shirts he wore were too feminine for her taste! This was quite unlike the Judeo/Christian cultures to the south, and some of the male dominated cultures of the Indian sub-continent where the man would kick the woman out with just the clothes and jewelry she had on at the time.

The symbolism of JERA - ᛃ is that of the year, the cycle of karma, and the fertility needed for the harvest. Agrarian people all over the world base their year on the solar equinoxes and solstices with specific lunar months and phases prescribed for such important events as planting a new field and collecting or harvesting food.

In reality, there is not one harvest, but several throughout the year. The first is around the spring equinox when the first new shoots, herbs, and vegetables come forth along with the migrations of fish, birds, and animals. The next harvest is around the first of summer when the first fields are planted and the early berries and fruits are harvested. Around the fall equinox, the planted fields are harvested along with nuts, late berries, and most grains. The final harvest of the year ends around the Winter solstice which is the hunter's harvest of game, late nuts, and sap. The only time where harvesting is really scarce in the far north is in the middle of winter, from January through March.

RUNIC STATES

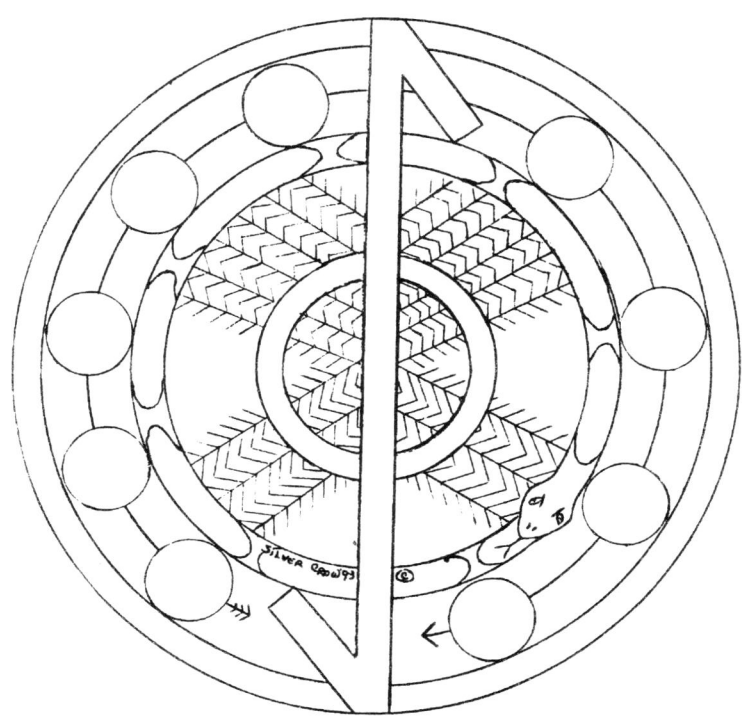

EIHWAR (E, 1)
(*EYE - are*)

13
YEW TREE
POLITICS
WORLD AXIS
COMMUNICATION
LIFE GIVER/SUSTAINER
COLOR - GREEN
DEFENSE
WEDNESDAY
PATIENCE

THE TREE OF COMMUNICATION

The ancient northern cultures make an interesting study in trees. The different cultures had different creation myths, but trees played prominent roles in most of them. In the Finnish creation tradition an oak over shadowed the world and had to be cut down for the sun to shine to the ground. Then the remaining trees were cut so there was room to allow the crops to grow. The only tree spared was the birch so the birds would have a place to nest.

In some traditions the world tree is an oak, in others it is an ash tree. When we speak of the tree of communication, it is the rune of the yew tree where Odhin hung to receive knowledge of the runes.

The rune of the yew is EIHWAR - ᛇ. The form is made of LAGUR - ᛚ up and LAGUR - ᛚ reversed; flow up to the heavens and flow down to the earth. Just as the yew tree is straight up with the branches lateral, the tap root is straight down with roots lateral.

In Shamanism, we work down a tree root or cave to reach the underworld to find the spirit helpers of the plant and animal worlds. We also work up a tree or mountain to jump into the clouds to reach the overworld for training and advice on spiritual matters from the archetype spirits. An evergreen tree such as the yew is preferred for this work. The rune also works for the communication within man, the subconscious to the conscious to the superconscious.

The home of this rune in a runecast is on the mental plane where it connects the spirit realm to the physical plane. Its most powerful position is in the present and mental since then it acts as a channel. There it can help the prayers from the past and physical reach the future and spiritual position, while at the same time it can conduct the answers from the past and spiritual to the future and physical. Meanwhile it forms a direct connection between the spiritual and physical in the present, a direct tie where the NOW gives you the power to make changes in your life.

The source of the word Wednesday in the English language is really muddled. The word derives from the old English and the Viking influence being WOTAN's day, another name for Odhin. However, the planetary influence is that of Mercury which is supposed to rule mentality, again a good connection to an attribute of Odhin, **but** the deity in the Norse pantheon which substitutes for Mercury is Loki, the God of Cunning, Treachery, and Chaos. So what rune is best for this day? There is no direct rune for Odhin according to some, though Edred Thorsson connects ANSUR - ᚠ with Loki and the inspiration of Odhin. Looking in the books on shamanism and the Kalevala, a relation is clearer. Mercury is the communication between the worlds, the Yggdrasil is the tree holding all the worlds, a way of communication between them, and tightly bound with Odhin. So the rune for this day should be that of the Yggdrasil, the yew tree, EIHWAR - ᛇ.

A straight grained wood, when dried the yew makes a superb bow for defense and hunting for animals, providing for the sustenance of life when the fields are barren. This also helps with developing the virtue of patience. This relationship to the bow is what ties it to the two close knit families it is in, that of PROTECTION, and that of LIFE.

In the protection family we see EIHWAR - ᛇ, defense, the guardian with the bow; with BERKANO - ᛒ, concealment; united with HAEGEL - ᚺ, banishment; with ELHAR - ᛦ, sanctuary; with OTHALA - ᛟ, a retreat; and with THURISAR- ᚦ, thorns. In the family of life, we group EIHWAR - ᛇ, sustenance; with BERKANO - ᛒ, life cycle; with LAGUR - ᛚ, life force; and with ELHAR - ᛦ, health. In both of these groups we find the three same runes: ELHAR - ᛦ, BERKANO - ᛒ, and EIHWAR - ᛇ. Protection is vital for life, and conflict is inherent in living.

Now, the conflict inherent in living can be incidental and accidental, or intentional. To minimize accidental conflict, good communication is a great benefit. In some instances the conflict can be at a level of kill or be killed, eat or be eaten or die of starvation. A thousand years ago when the runes were at their peak, such conflicts were seen every day without being hidden as they are today behind layers of packaging and marketing, a thin veneer of over population and civilization.

To expand on this, this rune could be considered a symbol for politics, where communication or words takes the place of swords in battles between countries or corporations. However, I would not use it for legal communications since TIWAR - ᛏ rules the aspects of jurisprudence and legal battles. I use this rune whenever communication is needed to smooth over difficulties, especially those resulting from differences of viewpoint.

Einstein proved everything is relative, and no two observers could view a single event since they cannot be in the same place at the same time. Whenever an event is observed, the observer participates in the event. When an event in the sub-atomic realm is observed, the observation changes either the position or the velocity of the event. Even so communication is relative, those attempting the communication do not have the same background and experiences so view the communication from different vantage points. Therefore the participants in a communication see two or more different communications, one for each participant.

RUNIC STATES

PERTHO (P)
(*PURR - tho*)

14
DICE CUP
ÓRLOG (FATES, PRIMAL LAWS)
SYNCHRONICITY
UNCERTAINTY
EVOLUTION
INITIATION
URANUS

WHEN LIFE IS A GAMBLE

The planet Uranus rules both inventiveness and unconventionality. The best rune for this planet is PERTHO - ⌐ which deals with gambling and fate.

The Norse and some of the other Germanic tribes did not see life as we do. Good luck and bad luck did not balance out, a man made his own breaks in life, except when the fates interfered and brought disruption to his plans or laid a geas on him.

When the runes were in use, life was always a gamble, disaster lurked around every corner. While unconventionality was frowned upon socially, inventiveness was often necessary to get out of the disasters that loomed. Even Odhin turned to Loki on many occasions for that little bit of cunning or inventiveness that was needed to save the Gods. Of course, many of those traps were the results of Loki's deeds in the first place, and a blood oath with Odhin was the only thing that kept the Gods from killing the trouble maker many times over. Unconventionality was the cause of many problems, but inventiveness was the cure.

This brings us to another part of PERTHO - ⌐, synchronicity. All the word really means is being in time or in step with what is going on around you, like a ballet troupe in a performance being in step with each other and in time to the music. However, it means much more in relation to the Örlog.

The Germanic tribes recognized a set of primal laws laying behind reality. A set of rules which allowed cause and effect to operate. In their myths, they had the fates to handle predestination using these laws known as the Örlog.

The ultimate in predestination was a geas, a curse so heavy you could not avoid it, and often would drive you mad in a single minded determination to carry it out. Slightly less onerous was a wyrd or fate that could be delayed or modified but not avoided entirely since the wyrd was the effect of your previous actions in this lifetime. When you were working entirely in accordance with these primal laws, going with the flow as it is said, things happened for you, a wild streak of luck or synchronicity. This required being in tune with your fate, and using your free will to make sure it happened.

The shape of PERTHO - ⌐ is that of a dice cup, or any other container used to hold lots for casting. A slightly concave shape to the sides of the cup ensures the cast is random, or at least that the dice are tumbling in the air. This connects the symbolism for this rune to chance and fate through the act of gambling.

Inventiveness provokes change which is either evolution or revolution, depending on the speed in which it works and the scope of the changes involved. As such, it is a tool of the fates for making changes, a way of the mysteries to force an issue of change, to force you into the initiatory cycle of changes in life.

In following a shaman's path, the initiate is attuned to the realms of the spirits and ordinary reality, capable of performing in both places by shifting consciousness in ways most people never try. In these states the shaman notices little things in the surroundings that other miss.

When tuned to these minutiae, the shaman begins to develop a state of synchronicity that sometimes is noticed by the people associating with the shaman. If the culture does not generally recognize the shaman's path, such as modern western society, those noticing the synchronicity remark on the incredible luck or good fortune of the shaman.

In a quantum mechanics viewpoint we can try to associate synchronicity with the mechanics but it is really a stretch to do so since no one felt necessary to try to define it mathematically. Instead, we will associate PERTHO - ᛈ with the uncertainty principle that is mathematically stated.

In simple terms this principle states that you can either know the location or the motion of an object, such as an atom, but not both at the same time. In order to determine a location at a point in time you must change or arrest it's motion. Conversely, to determine a motion, the observation is set up to ignore the location, but which traces the path of the motion.

Let's make it a bit easier. Try holding your eyes still and focus on a moving finger. It is not possible. However, if you move your eyes to track the finger, you can focus on the finger, but the background becomes blurred.

It is the same with the uncertainty principle in quantum mechanics. It is similar when you consider the changes in the life cycle brought on by PERTHO - ᛈ, you can either see the changes going on, or the position you are at in the life cycle. It is difficult to the point of impossibility to focus both on the change and the position at the same time. You must let one go to concentrate on the other.

Even the shaman does not hold two states of consciousness at the same time except in extremely rare cases, but develops the facility to change focus between them rapidly. Having learned to work in both, the shaman takes his memory and skills back and forth between states of consciousness.

RUNIC STATES

ELHAR (Z, R)
(*L – has*)

15
ELK
SWAN
LIFE
HEALTH
SANCTUARY
ASTRAL TRAVEL (SILVER CORD)

THE BUFFALO OF THE NORTH

Just about everyone in the United States knows that the buffalo or bison was the life's blood of the plains Indian tribes. What they may not have known was the U.S. government paid bounty on the bison with the specific intent of starving these tribes into submission and to force them onto the reservations. Given the incentive of the bounty and the approval of the government, the buffalo hunters decimated the herds.

The meat of the bison was used for food. The hide made shelter and clothes. The horns and bones were made into glue and tools. Finally the bison was ingrained in the myths and religious stories of the tribes.

The elk and the reindeer, depending on region you look at, were the buffalo of northern Europe. In as many ways, these animals were vital to the life and health of the tribes which lived near the Arctic circle as the Buffalo were to the American Indian of the great plains. No part of the animals was wasted, every part had a use. The Vikings and other traders of the Germanic tribes were eager to trade for the wealth of these animals.

In the folk tales and myths of a vast region where the Germanic tribes held sway there is references to the swan. Do you remember the stories of the swan maidens? Some variety of this story can be found from the isles of Great Britain to Finland. In most of these stories the swan is a form of spirit, like an elf, or enchanted maiden who can only remove their feathers for brief periods, normally to bathe in a remote lake.

ELHAR - ᛉ is the symbol for the elk and for the swan, and also for what these two animals represent. Since the swan form is assumed to fly away, this is a symbol for astral travel, and specifically for the silver cord which ties the astral body to the physical body. This is the symbol for the flying dreams we have as children, and some still have as adults. That is the reason the form of ELHAR - ᛉ having the form of a bird's foot print is rather appropriate.

ELHAR - ᛉ as the elk is a sign of life and health for the food it provided. It was also a symbol of the sanctuary and protection provided by the hides as traveling tents, and warm coats, and so is found in the group dealing with protection, as protection against the elements.

As far as modern symbology is concerned, ELHAR - ᛉ is a symbol for travel by air, be it aircraft or spacecraft such as the space shuttle. The study of the atmosphere and the weather are also in the realm of ELHAR - ᛉ in the form of the swan.

The groupings we find ELHAR - ᛉ in includes one of with two members for astral travel. ELHAR - ᛉ is the silver cord, while MANNAZ - ᛗ is the guardian and the bridge to the astral plane.

It is also in a group of runes for life. These include ELHAR - ᛉ as health; EIHWAR - ᛇ, as the sustenance of life in spiritual matters; LAGUR - ᛚ which is the water of life, or the mother's milk which feeds the child, often called life force; and BERKANO - ᛒ, the cycle of life and death.

Finally, it is also found in travel. ELHAR - ᛉ is the airplane or helicopter or any form of transportation through the air. RAIDHO - ᚱ is the car, the train, or the truck of land transportation. EHWAR - ᛗ is the rune for walking or riding a horse, motorcycle, or bicycle. The last rune is that for travel by ship or water as seen represented by the spar and mast of NAUDHIR - ᚾ.

RUNIC STATES

SOWHILO (S)
(so - WHEEL - o)

16
SUN
SOLAR WHEEL/CROSS
MAGICAL WILL
CHAKRAS
REGENERATION
WHOLENESS
COLOR - GOLD
SUNDAY
SUCCESS
LIGHTNING
ELECTRICITY

BASK IN THE SON SHINE

In the description of BERKANO - ᛒ I used a pun on the word son and sun in order to point out that the light of the life in a patriarchy is the son which will inherit. Many daughters can ruin a man who has to supply their dowries.

Linguistically, puns and other jokes very rarely translate well. The jokes are dependent on the cultures and what they find amusing while the puns only work when the words and languages are related. The pun used translates well between German and English due to their relations as languages derived from the common tongue of the Germanic tribes, and their repeated interactions later in their history.

Still on the linguistic topic, we look at SOWHILO - ᛋ, the rune of the sun. The spelling of this rune can vary from SOWELO to SOWHILO, the way I spell it here. The spelling I used puts the stress on the second syllable instead of the first, so - WHEEL - o. The position of the silent H changes the timing and stress of the second syllable.

The first meaning of this rune as the sun, connects to the meaning tied to it, that of wholeness, through the pun. It is the son that will inherit that makes the man complete in a patriarchy. The links to Sunday and the solar wheel comes from the name, and from being symbol for the sun. In astrology, the sun rules the identity so the person inherits the major personality traits of the symbol where the sun is located.

To tie in the regeneration meaning, examine the sun as it appears daily. In the day to day reappearance, there is no change to the sun's shape or size, the change only occurs with the seasons in the height above the horizon and the heat felt. The earth's bounty of plants reappear and regenerate with the lengthening of the sun's visibility in the spring. This regeneration would be easily noted by people with a tie to the land. This is the sun whose return we celebrate each spring in our Easter rituals.

The color associated with SOWHILO - ᛋ is the golden hue of sunshine. There are theories about the origin of the Germanic tribes which tie the volcano, the storm, and the sun as a major root of their religion. The volcano glowed at night because the sun rested there, and the lightning flashes above the mountain was bits of the sun escaping. Depending on what metal was mixed with pure gold, the color varies from the red of a sunrise to a yellowish or white gold of high noon. The colors of a volcano vary in the same way, the connection here is stronger than people who have never seen a volcano at night without city lights can ever know.

The grouping for light has the sun, SOWHILO - ᛋ; DAGAZ - ᛗ, the time when the sun rises; and WYRD -   for polarity, darkness and the night.

The shape of SOWHILO - ᛋ is the lightning bolt which is the sun breaking through the storm clouds or splitting the blackness of night asunder. With this lightning bolt is associated the modern concept of electricity. The sun releases a wide range of energies and forces from the atomic furnace that is its heart, so wide that to look at that for the tie on the quantum side is a futile effort. Instead we use its representation of lightning to provide a symbol meaningful to modern society.

With SOWHILO - ᛋ, you can see the four seasons in the solar wheel. For spring we can use DAGAZ - ᛗ or daybreak, for summer we use SOWHILO - ᛋ or sun, for the fall harvest we see JERA - ᛃ, and for winter's cold, ISA - I. This is the grouping of the year.

In the group of success we find two runes, TIWAR - ↑ and SOWHILO - ᛋ. The first is victory, success in a conflict. The conflict can be on the battlefield, in the courtroom, or a matching of wills with an adversary. At the risk of being monotonous, the success of SOWHILO - ᛋ can be tied back to the pun of the son. The birth of a baby is a feeling of success for both the mother and the father, but a son was felt much more keenly in the patriarchies. The flush of success here is for a task accomplished, a job well done, a troubling time or danger passed.

The last symbolic connection to be addressed here is that of the will and the chakras. The solar cross or Nordic solar wheel from which the form of SOWHILO - ᛋ can be derived, is the symbol of the esoteric magical will. The chakras are energy points in the astral body that are often portrayed as flowers in India's art. Most people who can see the chakras describe them as little swirling points of color in the aura resembling suns. When meditation allows someone to expand and work with the chakras, it is described as a flower opening from a bud, or a ball of light that expands outward from the body as it opens. In cases where the body's temperature needs to be raised, the chakra of the solar plexus is visualized to expand and become a small, warm sun.

RUNIC STATES

TIWAR (T)
(*TEA - r*)

17
TUESDAY
TESTING OF INITIATIONS
DISCRIMINATION
PERSERVERANCE
JUSTICE
EXPERIMENTAL METHOD
SPIRITUAL DISCIPLINE
VICTORY THRU SELF-SACRIFICE

TRIALS AND TRIBULATIONS

The rune TIWAR - ↑ is pronounced the same as the god Tyr which it represents. This is the same deity as Mars was for the Mediterranean, a one handed god of war. In the case of Tyr, he lost his hand as a sacrifice to chain the Fenris wolf. Since Fenris could not break the dainty golden chain, he bit off the hand which had been placed in his mouth as a surety. So there are two connections in this one act for our consideration, that of sacrifice and discipline.

In the areas of northern Europe of the time of the runes, there was no real trial by a jury of your peers. You were subject to the court of the king, or of the nobles appointed by him. The closest to a jury trial was trial by combat, if you were of a sufficiently noble status to be able to demand one. Therefore, this derivation places justice in the realm of warfare, and so in the province of Tyr.

For many, the meanings of this rune stops with victory through sacrifice, the judicial aspects, and with spiritual discipline. However, with the warrior aspect, comes perseverance, and with the judicial comes discrimination. We can easily find one more connection, that of a day of the week. The day for this rune's discussion is Tuesday. The first connection is that this is Tyr's day so we have a direct connect to the rune TIWAR - ↑. Then, by association we know that Tyr is the planet Mars. So the planetary influence is of drive and determination.

As I worked on this rune, I began to see that a few details were being overlooked. According to some writers just about every male deity is Odhin in disguise, or an aspect of him. Tyr is not one of the deities constantly in the myths, but to lump all males as splinter psyches of Odhin is not a theory I can buy into.

Finally a piece fell into place. In *DUNE*, the Bene Gesserit have the test of the Gom Jabbar; the hand of the tested is placed in a black box which directly stimulates the nerves. The hand feels like it is being burned off in a fire. The test is designed to see if the person being tested can overcome the animal instinct to pull the hand out. The Bene Gesserit thought a human would stay in the trap to destroy the trapper, performing a needed sacrifice for the good of the community.

TIWAR - ↑ is the rune of tribulation, the test of the rite of passage. The test which determines if the candidate can overcome the difficulties and muster the courage, perseverance, and discrimination to handle the powers and abilities of a new position in life. Tyr is the master who conducts the test, the impartial judge who allows no miscarriage of justice.

Here we find the two aspects from which we can derive the symbolism for modern science. As the ruler of testing and impartial judgment, TIWAR - ↑ could be said to rule the scientific method itself. The trial and error, unbiased experiments with impartial observation is the basis for this derivation. Experiments must have repeatable, verifiable results, and any statistical analysis of the results must be free of biased statistical analysis.

In *The Old Norse Sagas*, Halvdan Koht tells us that the impression we have of the legality of trial by combat is a bunch of romantic hogwash, probably invented by the church bishops to discredit the earlier Pagan customs. In his studies he found no trace of such a concept in the legal codes. Quite to the contrary, when a person was killed in a duel, a lawsuit often resulted to obtain a blood or were guild being assessed. This being a fine paid to the surviving kin for loss of use of the person. However, in these times, the sheriff was not called to deal with all crimes, justice was a civil case for the wronged party to pursue. Thus what we now let the courts settle, the victim could settle the account in blood. In other words a trial by combat, and not necessarily in a duel on the field of honor.

In order to make it easier to identify which meaning of TIWAR - ↑ is meant in a reading, TIWAR - ↑ is linked to the following groups of runes. In the family for success, there are just two runes; SOWHILO - ϟ meaning success, and TIWAR - ↑ implying victory through sacrifice. In the realm of the spirit; TIWAR - ↑ is discipline, ANSUR - ᚠ is knowledge, and RAIDHO - ᚱ is development.

RUNIC STATES

BERKANO (B)
(*BURR - can - o*)

18
BIRCH
GROWTH
EARTH MOTHER
EARTH SCIENCES
BIRTH/LIFE/DEATH CYCLE
(REBIRTH)
CONCEALMENT/PROTECTION

WITHIN LIFE, THE GODDESS

In the shape of BERKANO - ᛒ everyone can recognize the breasts of the Goddess. But hidden within are the flag shape of WUNJO - ᚹ, joy or the clan banner; the lightning bolt of the sun or success, SOWHILO - ᛋ; ISA - I, the straight line of ice; spiritual development found in the form of RAIDHO - ᚱ; KENAZ - ᚲ, the fire of regeneration; and LAGUR - ᛚ, the upwelling waters and the flow of life.

We will start with the shape instead of placing it at the end due to all of the other runes that are hidden in it's shape. In this aspect it is the most complex of all the runes. As to difficulty of carving, it is a toss up as to whether PERTHO - ᛈ or BERKANO - ᛒ is the most complex as both have a single cross grain back with four angles off of the main cut. In PERTHO - ᛈ there are only three runes hidden, half of the number found in BERKANO - ᛒ.

Traditionally, BERKANO - ᛒ refers to the Birch Tree, and has the meaning of growth or rebirth. Again, as in the shape, there is more to the meanings attributed to BERKANO - ᛒ than is first apparent. The Birch is one of the sacred trees of the Germanic tribes. According to the Finnish mythology, Vainamoinen left a single birch tree standing when he cleared the ground for the planting of crops so the eagles and other birds could have a place to perch and build nests. This wise act earned him the eternal friendship of the birds.

As a wood, birch is of moderate hardness and has straight, relatively close grain. This makes it easy to work with, yet valuable for making furniture and utensils. It does not have the hardness necessary to make tools which get used and abused. Pushed to the limit birch does not hold up too well, however it is admirably suited to making boxes and bowls. As a box protects its contents, and a mother her child, so BERKANO - ᛒ is a rune with protective properties.

In making the healing bind rune I found all the physical healing properties in BERKANO - ᛒ. This is appropriate since growth and healing are two shades of the same color. Examining some of the varieties of evergreen we see that the cones holding the seed will not open except by the heat of a fire below. The growth of the new trees is tied to the healing of the fire damage.

There is a bit of folk wisdom saying everything either grows or dies, that to stop growing is to stagnate and to begin to die. Growth is life, and life is growth, the two are closely intertwined. So BERKANO - ᛒ is life and growth;

healing and rebirth; derived basically from the accepted and traditional definitions of the rune.

This leaves one major use for this rune not yet covered, the Goddess. Besides the shape, what gives rise to the psyche's labeling this as such? We could start by asking which runes are attributed to goddesses by Thorsson and others of a Heathen bent. There are only two. Freya shows up as KENAZ - <, Freya being the Goddess of love. BERKANO - ᛒ is the earth goddess, the complement to ING - ◊ as the earth god, both being the repositories of fertility, but not seen in the normal pantheon of the *Edda*.

These two goddesses show up in the runes in the company of five gods. Both goddesses show attributes of passion and fertility, while the gods are for fertility, war, justice, cunning, and strength. Not exactly balanced, but then we are talking of a patriarchal culture after all, the only use they saw for a woman is to have male children and take care of the housework. These runes show the feminine in two aspects; that of the maid - Freya, and of the mother - Berkano.

As I said at the beginning, the shape of this rune, BERKANO - ᛒ, is that of the breasts of the goddess of motherhood. LAGUR - ᛚ is found hidden in the shape, the upwelling and flow of the waters (milk) of life. A mother's breast is a haven for the youth, a shelter and sanctuary for comfort when the cares of the world are too great. WUNJO - ᚹ, the clan banner is raised by all the sons she can bear. KENAZ - < is both the fire of regeneration, and the maiden she used to be. SOWHILO - ᛋ, is the sun, uh, spell that son, that shines in a man's life. ISA - I, can be the ice of winter and cold shoulder she gives. RAIDHO - ᚱ, is the wagon or sled of the matrimonial elopement. Surely you don't think she is working for your spiritual development, do you?

Now that the slice of patriarchal thinking is done, let's try to straighten out some of the trash of the last three paragraphs. As the mother goddess form, BERKANO - ᛒ is a refuge for hurts, a way of healing both the soul and the body. A little TLC (tender LOVING care) is the milk of human kindness, fostering growth and healing. As the Earth Goddess, BERKANO - ᛒ, is both nurturing and healing, as well as the lady of the crops. Fertility to keep the clan alive with food and with new men and women to carry on the traditions of the clan. Any dog daring to deride the importance of these, and thus the importance of BERKANO -- ᛒ will be used for target practice forthwith by every person in the clan.

What is the value of this rune? Ask what was the importance of women in the Germanic tribes. The maidens were a dowry and future mother. The main value of any woman was held in the child bearing and child rearing mother. Not only was the fertility vital to the continued existence of the tribe, but the healing knowledge they acquired made those surviving the child bearing years valuable as well, even if now barren. Keeping the tribe healthy is almost as important as bearing new members of the tribe.

Ask also what is the value of a mother? That is the key to understanding this rune. For the Birch is the mother tree where the birds nest. It is the first tree in some orders of the Druid tree circles and calendars. A child will answer the question in a manner different than a youth, and still different than and adult. It would be fair to say that BERKANO - ᛒ is the mother of the runes, and even though not strictly in accordance with the *Edda*, the mother of the gods.

As a modern symbol, I still give it all the properties associated with motherhood, but in addition to the Earth Goddess, give it the earth sciences such as geology and ecology. You could add biology and all the other life sciences, but then its meaning would be too vague, there would be too many possibilities as to what was meant. So as the Earth Goddess, Gaia, BERKANO - ᛒ could be added to the list of planets as the symbol for the Earth.

RUNIC STATES

EHWAR (E)
(*EARS*)

19
HORSE'S EARS
MOVEMENT
TRANSITION
TRUST IN MARRIAGE
HARMONIOUS DUALITY
FERTILITY
SENSUALITY

THE EARS OF THE HORSE

Once again I want to start this discussion with the shape of the rune. Some would say it is the letter M, but in meditating on the meanings of this rune, it is easy to get the source of the shape. From the rider's position, this rune is the ears of the horse when pricked forward.

For EHWAR - ᛖ I left the spelling as it was, and simply let the HW be silent, drawing the pronunciation out a little. The traditional meaning is the horse itself, but since the shape came from the ears I add it in. The main discussion for EHWAR - ᛖ is on the topic of the role of the horse to nomadic warrior cultures. From this most of the meanings are easily derived.

Ever hear of the expression "Hung like a horse"? Obvious fertility connection there. Next, in the same line, why do girls enjoy riding horses so much? When asked, most will talk about the strong muscular animal, trust, feelings of flying or floating. Psychologists will have a lot to say about sublimation of emotions, substitutions for relations with males, or subconscious sexual symbols, i.e. riding the male, controlling the male, etc. Some of the less inhibited will admit that the sensuality of riding just turns them on.

This leads to some of the characteristics of the horse the girls are relating to, and which made them invaluable to the nomads. When trained, the horse develops a close partnership with its rider based on trust. This relationship is closer than many marriages, the horse willing to do anything to please its rider. When the rider is properly trained, the horse and rider are as one, subtle shifts in weight direct the horse, and provide balance for both. This is the trust that should be in all marriages, the harmonious duality where two become one.

The ears of the horse are more expressive than some peoples faces. When you talk to the horse, many times it will swing an ear back to hear you better. When the horse pays attention to something it likes, or is interested in the ears are pricked forward forming the shape of the rune EHWAR - ᛖ. When upset the ears are flat back across the top of the head.

These attributes as well as its greater strength made the horse invaluable to the nomadic tribes. After the invention of the chest harness and yoke, the greater mass and strength increased its value. Before then it could only be used to carry light loads. The oxen could pull much greater weights, and was more tractable, but also slower and less intelligent. Next to the dog, it was questionably the most valuable domesticated animal. Questionably because some debate on the edible ox, sheep with wool, fowls, and such.

But for the nomad the horse made them much more mobile. The oxen could pull the cart or wagon while the scouts and warriors in the chariots used the horses to range ahead and to flank the tribe in its movement. Plus, it made it easier to leave a small detachment to follow the cattle herds and flocks. This detachment was able to range back with the flocks or herds, and run up to the main wagons when needed much easier than walking.

So the horse supplied movement to the nomads. In modern terms EHWAR - M would also be a motorcycle, often called an iron horse. It can also signify a transition between states or stages in a cycle.

This is also the transition between stages of a chemical or atomic reaction. Bonds between atoms stretch when energy is added, finally break, then new bonds are formed and the reaction is completed. EHWAR - M is that brief, or not so brief, time when the bond has broken, but a new bond has not formed and the atom or molecule is unstable, looking for its complement to stabilize it.

In its concepts of marriage and harmony, EHWAR - M might be placed in the group for binding with GEBO - X and WUNJO - P, but the fit is not good. It is a member of the group for travel with RAIDHO - R, NAUDHIR - ✦, and ELHAR - Y. Finally it is found in the life cycles group due to its being a transition between states of the cycle.

RUNIC STATES

MANNAZ (M)
(*MAN - as*)

20
HUMANITY
MODESTY
EGO
DIVINE IN MAN
BLOOD BROTHER
CLAN
ASTRAL TRAVEL
BRIFROST THE BRIDGE
HEIMDALL
MIRROR IMAGES

THE CLAN OF MANKIND

The first rune in the grouping of runes related to mankind is the rune for blood kin, MANNAZ - ᛗ. A broad meaning would be humanity, but going a step closer to the individual it refers to the group of people with a blood tie (a clan), and closer to the individual, it stands for the ego of the individual. On a spiritual level it normally refers to the divine in man, the divine spark. If considered on a mental level it is the ego, or in a case of extreme ego, when reversed it counsels us to cultivate modesty and to be introspective.

The form of this rune can be traced back through many cultures which did not use runes. They had an ideograph of two hands clasping each other with an accepted meaning of friendship or brotherhood. For the rune shape, MANNAZ - ᛗ consists of two banners (WUNJO - ᚹ) facing each other, similar to the two hands. When reversed beware the betrayal by friends or broken contracts of business *friends*.

The form is that of WUNJO - ᚹ with the tip of the banner on a mirror. This is known as bilateral symmetry in biological terms. Most forms of life show bilateral symmetry or a combination of bilateral and radial symmetry. This concept is important to life at the chemical level as well. A normal sugar we use for food is not symmetrical. When the mirror image of the sugar is ingested, the body cannot use it as food, instead it is passed out as so much garbage.

The rune MANNAZ - ᛗ is linked to two groups. The first is that for the clan where it shows the people of the clan along with WUNJO - ᚹ, the clan's banner, and OTHALA - ᛟ, the clan's house and land.

The only other link is found in the grouping for astral travel. In this group MANNAZ - ᛗ being the guardian of the bridge, Heimdall, as well as the bridge to the astral planes itself. The other rune for astral travel is ELHAR - ᛦ, the jump off to and return from the astral planes. One of the pitfalls most people experience with astral travel is that of forgetting what occurred. When the astral form repositions itself in the body, clear memory of the trip often vanishes in most people with the only memory being a vague dream of flying or falling. This forgetting can be represented by MANNAZ - ᛗ, guarding the secrets of astral travel as Heimdall. Any of the secrets that might be damaging to the fragile balance of the ego are censored and forgotten.

RUNIC STATES

LAGUR (L)
(*LAG - er*)

21
WATER
FLOW
CLEANSING
WAVE MECHANICS
LIFE FORCE
GROWTH
LEEK
SUBCONSCIOUS

THE DRINK OF THE GODS

When you cut through all the meanings attributed to this rune one thing stands out, it refers to liquids and the properties of liquids. We start with water which can include lakes, ponds, streams, and rivers. Water that stands, or water that flows. Water that cleans and nourishes, vital for life and growth.

How do you turn water into food? Let a mother convert it for her young, ferment it with fruit, or ferment it with grains. In any event you have food to drink; milk, any variety of wines, or a larger group from grains such as beer, mead, ale, lager, and stout, the name depending on the grains used and fermentation method.

The three drinks mentioned in the *Kalevala* are milk, mead, and beer. Depending on story and version of the *Edda*, the drinks mentioned are mead and milk, though this varies greatly at the discretion of the translator. For the most part, the drink of the gods is described as a mead or ale.

One of the other foods vital to life in the north, and growing best where water is plentiful is the leek, a mild form of onion, not growing bulbous, but straight and long. The prize winning leeks now are as thick as your wrist and as long as your forearm. Most of the leeks carried by the grocers are only a little smaller in diameter. Without the variety of vegetables available to us through grocers and national trucking companies, native foods such as the leek become very important in supplying vitamins and minerals important to maintaining good health.

In classical physics wave mechanics refer to the properties of water as a medium for transmitting waves. In quantum physics this term refers to these same rules and laws as they apply to the electromagnetic spectrum and the sub-atomic pieces which create or act as wave forms. This is the best way of energy transmission, even electricity in a wire can be thought of as a wave form and the wire as a medium.

Here is a theoretical question which is not answered by the physicists. If wave forms are defined by travel through a medium, how can electromagnetic wave forms travel through space from star to star in a vacuum? They have run tests to disprove the existence of ether, but using light split between mirrors on mountain tops does not effectively represent the not quite vacuum of space. I say not quite vacuum because there has been proven to be atomic and molecular hydrogen as well as dust in interstellar space. If the only way for such a transmission is due to the particle/wave form dichotomy of quantum physics, then when we lose the medium in space the wave form properties should be lost, leaving only the particulate properties. So light as well as all of the waves here in the earth's atmosphere where we live can be represented by LAGUR - ʟ.

The form of LAGUR - ʟ is similar to the drinking straw from a juice box. This is also the way the leek's top tips over for the outer leaves, and that of the hand pumps that are used on many older wells. This form is also the way light bounces off a mirror, the wave form bending as it reflects off the silvered back of the mirror.

In the discussion of BERKANO - ʙ, we mention that LAGUR - ʟ is a representation of the milk of life. Above we linked the water to the milk and the mead, the drinks of the gods, and thus to this rune LAGUR - ʟ. The shape ties in to wave mechanics, as it does to the leek, another food of the watery places. In all this, we come back to nourishment, growth, and to life, even the very force of life.

One more attribute to LAGUR - ʟ lies in the esoteric realm of dream interpretation. Water symbolizes the subconscious in the practice of dream interpretation. So on the mental level, LAGUR - ʟ can be the dark waters of the subconscious.

RUNIC STATES

ING (NG)
(*ING*)

22
EARTH FATHER
POTENTIAL ENERGY
SATURDAY
GESTATION
COMPLETION OF BEGINNING

THE FORGOTTEN GOD

In the study of BERKANO - ᛒ, we see that ING - ◊ and BERKANO - ᛒ are companions, the male and female aspects of the earth's fertility. This is very much like the God and Goddess of many Pagan religions. For the most part, the Goddess rules the crops in the field, while the God rules the prey of the hunt and the wild woods. These are the deities of the more peaceful agrarian people.

If you would consider BERKANO - ᛒ as the mother of the Gods, then ING - ◊ is the father, and as such would be the equivalent of Saturn to the Mediterranean people, and the ruler of Saturday. Saturn is supposed to be leader of the Titans, and the father of Zeus, the leader of the new Gods of Olympus. This would correspond to the father of Odhin, Borr. Though not truly correct, this is approximately the same as ING - ◊, the Earth Father, who is much like Saturn who is a patron of farmers.

Let's take a quick look at the gods of the *Edda*. Wotan, one of three brothers, rules a pantheon including eight sons, most of these are devoted to the principles of war or of justly ruling the conquered. All males and many of the females in the pantheon are expected to fight and die in Ragnarok, except for the blind God Balder, killed through Loki's deceit and trickery. Is it not apropos that the God of peace and light was the victim of the God of cunning? Just look at the corporate raiders of today, buying companies to skim the retirement funds for their own inflated standard of living. There are more gods for types of warfare in this pantheon than any other; strength, trickery, blind brute force, justice in battle, as well as normal skill of arms.

What does this tell us? The people who worshiped the pantheon of the *Edda*, the normal Norse mythology, were a nomadic, warrior society who conquered everyone in their path and they had Gods to match. When they ran into the Atlantic ocean, they were forced to settle in Germany, Norway, Sweden, and the general area. Soon they took to ships instead of horses and went a-Viking, conquering the sea and the peoples settled near the seas. They settled Iceland and Greenland, parts of the British Isles, and even had colonies on the North American continent.

In the normal descriptions of the runes, we find a god of the conquered peoples, ING - ◊, but very little else of him. By all accepted definitions, he was the earth father, the male fertility god. As such, his fertility act is the end of the beginning, then the female carries the young, and signifies the waiting of gestation, where the male has little else to do until the time of birth.

The shape of ING - ◊ is either a diamond smaller than all the other runes, or with the sides extended to make it the same height as the other runes, a later development according to R. I. Page. The shape of ING - ◊ is found in one other rune, that of OTHALA - ᛉ, the clan house which is ING - ◊ over a roof or mantle of a hearth. In JERA - ᛃ, the cycle of the year or harvest, it is possible to see ING - ◊ cut in half and the halves separated if you care to stretch a possibility.

Again we drift back to the point of why ING - ◊ is the forgotten god. At first glance, ING - ◊ is not in the pantheon of the *Edda*, and his very nature is alien to it. However, when you read the other works and stutdies of the time, Freyr is often referred to as Freyr Ing. This link shows once more the fertility aspect and the God of the Field mentioned above.

As a god of the conquered tribe, ING - ◊ would be the replaced god of the ancestors, the god of the clan house or clan hearth. As the early Christians show us, it is easier to displace the earlier gods by either naming them as saints or demons, than it is to deny their existence. The tribes which brought in the *Edda* may have been well aware of this, and left the escape valves of BERKANO - ᛒ and ING - ◊ for the earlier deities they replaced with their pantheon. Let the defeated god have his name, or a sign with a different name, as in Freyr Ing, and in a few years the new generation will have forgotten him.

As the fertility god, he could be reckoned as the yearly sacrifice of the king to assure the harvest, and make way for a new consort to the Goddess if the culture was one that practiced the yearly sacrificial regicide of some Goddess religions. This would also tie into the period of gestation and waiting from the time of the regicide to the rebirth of the king, even if it was only a day or so.

In modern psychology, the concepts of this rune is one of potential, of waiting to be. The male has potential, but without the female cannot bring forth any fruit, and then still it is her doing the work. The appropriate energy for this rune is potential energy; the energy of a wound spring or a boulder sitting on a cliff. Once movement starts it is either mechanical or kinetic energy, but as long as everything is still and in stasis, it is only the potential for energy.

Also, if the tie to the ancient regicide sacrifices is valid it is one that modern man is not comfortable with, a God modern culture would sooner forget, so it does not have to be reminded of its bloody past, truly a forgotten god.

There is another forgotten god that is relevant to be mentioned here. Mithra was a god of the Persian and Romans, equated to the sacred, sacrificial bull or ox (URUZ - ᚢ). As the consort of the Mother Goddess, he eventually replaced her as the primary deity. A favorite of the Roman legions, the worship of Mithra was brought to the lands of the Germanic tribes before the earliest surviving runes.

Mithra was worshipped in natural caves, buried temples, and artificial caves. The shape of Ing could well be related to the the entrance of these buried temples. Also, both were worshipped as gods of fertility.

RUNIC STATES

DAGAZ (D, TH)
(*DAG - as*)

23
DAY
BREAKTHROUGH
POLARITY
VISIBLE SPECTRUM

THE END...OR THE BEGINNING

There is quite a bit of confusion when you study DAGAZ - ᛞ. On the surface it is quite straight forward. The literal translation is day. This relatively straight forward definition puts it in the group for light with SOWHILO - ᛋ the sun. It also puts it in the group for time with WYRD -   and JERA - ᛃ making the times of day, month, and year.

More specifically DAGAZ - ᛞ refers to daybreak or nightfall, the time when the sun is setting or rising, the beginning of night or the beginning of day. As such it means a break in the cycle either the end of the cycle or a fresh beginning. Like daybreak, which is it, the end of night or the beginning of day? This question can get into really involved philosophy. It also brings out the concept of polarity, actually a balancing act. Day is contrasted and balanced against night; light against darkness. This is why it is found in the life cycle as the last rune for the breakthrough, the end of the cycle.

If we use Alexander's solution to the Gordian knot for this problem, we say it is both an ending and a beginning, yet neither for a cycle is a circle without a beginning or an end. Just endless changes in a lifetime, one step done, another to commence. The senior graduating high school becomes a freshman entering college or an entry level drudge in the work force. There is a change of status, but was there any change in the person? Very likely not. That would come later.

In view of our knowledge of quantum physics, DAGAZ - ᛞ is assigned to the visible light portion of the electromagnetic spectrum. This may extend a little beyond what you can see into either the ultraviolet or infrared portions. Different people and animals have slightly different ranges of vision. Most people can distinguish as little as one photon of a certain wavelength of green, but may need over a thousand photons to distinguish a deep red or blue light. People who use monochrome computer monitors or are constantly looking at one color can become temporarily colorblind to that shade. Normally the vision will correct itself after a month or two if this is the cause.

The shape of DAGAZ - ᛞ is very rarely found in nature, the hourglass on the black widow spider, and the formation of the arms in Thorsson's standing meditation with the right hand on the left shoulder and vice versa with the elbows down at the side. This is the position of the Egyptian mummy and esoteric masters, a position of closing. It could also be GEBO - X or KENAZ - ᚲ mirrored between ISA - I.

RUNIC STATES

In all of these cases it is the snake that grabs its own tail in its mouth, then twists itself into the ellipse of eternity. Opposites sitting balanced in agreement, not warfare.

RUNIC STATES

OTHALA (O)
(O - tha - la)

24
ANCESTRAL PROPERTY
SEPARATION
CLAN HOUSE
INBORN QUALITIES
RETREAT
FREEDOM
PROSPERITY
LEVERAGE PRINCIPLE

THE HOUSE OF THE CLAN

The last rune in the grouping of mankind is that for the clan house, OTHALA - ᚨ. Besides the physical clan house and lands, this rune can be the qualities of the people of the clan such as freedom loving, quick to anger, gentle, red hair, blue eyes, et cetera. Basically, any identifying mark of the clan. It can also be an area for retreat, a feeling of safety, or protected area. Finally, though seemingly unrelated, this rune can be a symbol for prosperity or separation as when a young adult leaves the house to begin self-directed life.

This rune's form is that of a roof over GEBO - X, the rune for harmony or a union of many in one. Also, as described in the discussion on ING - ◊, it can be the form of the roof where ING - ◊ rests. The form of the roof is that of KENAZ - <, a fire or torch, which could be the hearth of the house. Thus this rune is one for many sharing a fire, hearth, or roof as one. The enforced harmony of a shared hearth in the cold northern climate's winter can explain many of the qualities attributed to this rune. The connection to an associated meaning of prosperity is very possibly the result of the work accomplished in the clan house in winter making trade items.

The logic of the paragraph above is found in unrelated anthropological studies. In ancient Chinese the ideogram or sign for trouble was two women under one roof. Instead of a negative view, GEBO - X takes the positive view of harmony instead of dissension in closed quarters. The second study was where the Native American tribes normally called the period in January and February the moon of the clacking stones since this was the time when it was so cold out that everyone stayed in as much as possible. The people used this time for wood carving, flint knappery (the clacking stones) and other time consuming activities creating tools for the spring and summer when they would be out and following other pursuits.

Besides being the final rune in the clan grouping with WUNJO - ᛈ and MANNAZ - ᛗ, OTHALA - ᚨ can be located in two other groupings.

OTHALA - ᚨ is in the mancrafted article grouping which contains THURISAR - ᚦ representing the hammer of the smith, SOWHILO - ᛋ which is the wheel, WUNJO - ᛈ the clan's banner, OTHALA - ᚨ as the house, KENAZ - < which is the torch, RAIDHO - ᚱ the wagon, NAUDHIR - ᚾ which is the mast of the ships, and PERTHO - ᛈ which is the dice cup.

The other group for OTHALA - ᛟ is that of the life cycles:

HAEGEL - ᚺ		- disruption of the old
KENAZ - ᚲ		- opening for the new
NAUDHIR - ᚾ		- true need or readiness
FEHU - ᚠ		- a beckoning or prayer
ING - ᛜ		- gestation
URUZ - ᚢ		- the new pattern to come
PERTHO - ᛈ		- taking a gamble with the Órlog
ANSUR - ᚨ		- inspiration
OTHALA - ᛟ		- separation
EHWAR - ᛖ		- movement or transition
RAIDHO - ᚱ		- journey of change
BERKANO - ᛒ		- birth of change
DAGAZ - ᛞ		- breakthrough.

In the time we are dealing with when we discuss the runes, there are major differences from modern times. Each person had a set of expectations and a place from birth right. This also included a belonging to family, land, and clan. Cousins and relationships we consider distant were still vital. A failure in responsibility to relations could result in ostracism, and that could be a death sentence in the wilds.

As an example, at one time I was forced to leave my job for refusing to steal for the company, and for reporting my supervisor for doing so after repeated attempts to stop the practice by following approved company channels. I was warned about not being a team player, then officially ostracized. My actions of quitting instead of knuckling under finally got the attention of top management. After I left, the company cleaned up its act.

This story is told to bring up an interesting observation: In order to catalyze change you must be willing to walk the edge, step outside of the norms, and risk alienation and ostracism from the people you are working with (MANNAZ - ᛗ). As Archimedes said of his work on the principle of the lever, given a place to stand he could move the world. But you must step off the world to move it! OTHALA - ᛟ stands for the principle of leverage, one of the first discovered, and a basis for all science that followed.

RUNIC STATES

The three runes in the family of mankind, MANNAZ - ᛗ, WUNJO - ᚹ, and OTHALA - ᛟ are mainly about you, your relationships, and your family. They are also about your dreams and your work.

RUNIC STATES

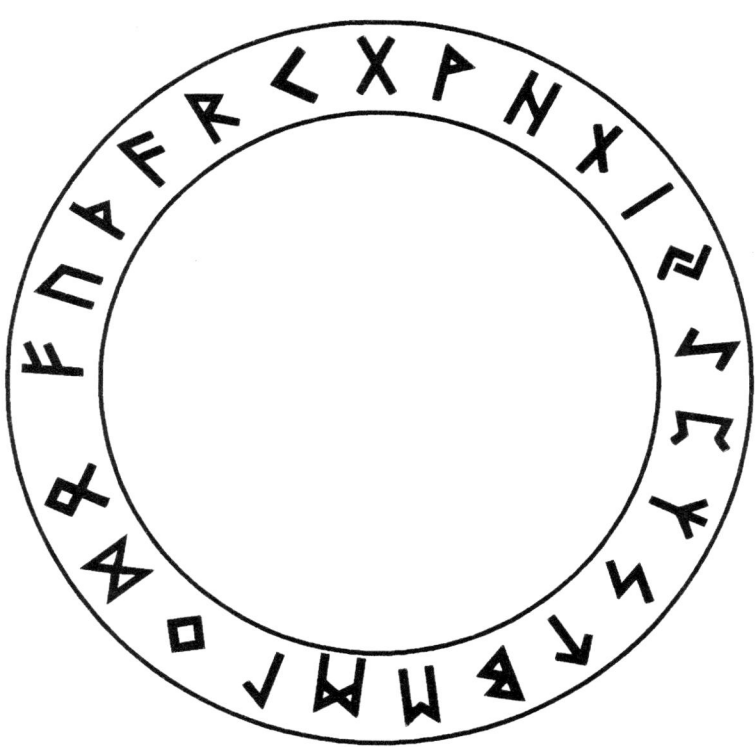

RUNIC STATES

Chapter 4: SYSTEMS AND STRUCTURES

RUNES, NUMBERS, AND OTHER ASPECTS

The key to understanding the runes as a system constructed in today's symbols and meanings is to place them where you can see them easily, and where the links between them can be viewed. This first section of this chapter is the information of short phrases and meanings for the runes as individuals as well as their numeric and alphabetic correspondences. This list is a table like I used in working on the first step in forming the family groupings for understanding this symbology system.

WYRD

0
DESTINY
SHON'JIR
DARKNESS
TAO, THE VOID
THE SHAMAN, WISE WOMAN
MONTH
COLOR - BLACK
MONDAY
THE MOON
SUBCONSCIOUS
WISDOM OF ODHIN

FEHU (F)

1
CATTLE
MONEY
POSSESSIONS
HEALING ENERGY (NOURISHMENT)
PRIMAL EXPANSION MOTION
PRAYER OR BLESSING

RUNIC STATES

URUZ (U, V)

2
OXEN
PASSAGE
MATTER TO COME
PATTERN'S FORCE
WISDOM
OPPORTUNITY IN LOSS
STRENGTH

THURISAR (TH)

3
THORN
MJOLLNIR
THURSDAY
GATEWAY
PROJECTED, APPLIED POWER
KINETIC ENERGY
VECTORS
NON-ACTION

ANSUR (A)

4
MESSENGER
LOKI
ANIMATION
INSPIRATION
SPIRIT POWER AND KNOWLEDGE
SONG AND POETRY
COMMUNICATION
NEPTUNE

RAIDHO (R)

5
WAGON
JOURNEY
DIVINE LAW AND ORDER
GOOD ADVICE/JUDGMENT
SPIRITUAL DEVELOPMENT
RHYTHM AND DANCE
MECHANICAL ENERGY

RUNIC STATES

KENAZ (K, C)

6
TORCH
OPENING
CONTROLLED FIRE
REGENERATION THROUGH
    SACRIFICE
ARTISTS CREATION
HUMANITY
PASSION/LUST (FREYA)
FRIDAY
COLOR - RED
EXOTHERMIC REACTIONS
SUB-ATOMIC BONDS
BREATH

GEBO (G)

7
GIFT
WEDDING
HOSPITALITY
TWO/MANY IN ONE
ECSTASY
PSYCHIC UNION
PLATONIC LOVE (PARTNERSHIP)

WUNJO (W)

8
JOY
HOPE
HARMONIC PRINCIPLE
NEW ENERGY
CLAN BANNER
FELLOWSHIP
HARMONIOUS BINDING
SYMPATHETIC ATTRACTION

RUNIC STATES

HAEGEL (H)

9
HAIL
DISRUPTION
PRIMAL SEED
RUNE MOTHER
PROTECTION AND BANISHMENT
RADICAL DISCONTINUITY
ELEMENTAL POWER

NAUDHIR (N)

10
COMPULSION
NEED
FATES' POWER
RESISTANCE
SHIP'S MAST
CONSTRAINT
CAUSE/EFFECT
WILL DIRECTED ACTION

ISA (I)

11
ICE
COLD
PRIMAL MATTER
COLOR - WHITE
STILLNESS
IDENTITY
ENDOTHERMIC REACTIONS
PATIENCE
PLUTO
INERTIA

JERA (J, Y)

12
YEAR
HARVEST
CYCLE
KARMA
FERTILITY (FREYR)

EIWHAR (E, I)

13
YEW TREE
WORLD AXIS
COMMUNICATION
LIFE GIVER/SUSTAINER
DEFENSE
COLOR - GREEN
POLITICS
PATIENCE
WEDNESDAY

PERTHO (P)

14
DICE CUP
ÓRLOG (FATES, PRIMAL LAWS)
SYNCHRONICITY
UNCERTAINTY
EVOLUTION
INITIATION
URANUS

ELHAR (Z, R)

15
ELK
SWAN
LIFE
HEALTH
SANCTUARY
ASTRAL TRAVEL (SILVER CORD)

RUNIC STATES

SOWHILO (S)

16
SUN
SOLAR WHEEL/CROSS
MAGICAL WILL
CHAKRAS
REGENERATION
WHOLENESS
COLOR - GOLD
SUNDAY
SUCCESS
LIGHTNING
ELECTRICITY

TIWAR (T)

17
TYR
TUESDAY
TESTING OF INITIATIONS
DISCRIMINATION
PERSEVERANCE
JUSTICE
EXPERIMENTAL METHOD
SPIRITUAL DISCIPLINE
VICTORY THRU SELF-SACRIFICE

BERKANO (B)

18
BIRCH
GROWTH
EARTH MOTHER
EARTH SCIENCES
BIRTH/LIFE/DEATH CYCLE
CONCEALMENT/PROTECTION

RUNIC STATES

EHWAR (E)

19
HORSE'S EARS
MOVEMENT
TRANSITION
TRUST IN MARRIAGE
HARMONIOUS DUALITY
FERTILITY/SENSUALITY

MANNAZ (M)

20
HUMANITY
EGO
DIVINE IN MAN
MODESTY
BLOOD BROTHER
CLAN
ASTRAL TRAVEL
BRIFROST THE BRIDGE
HEIMDALL
MIRROR IMAGES

LAGUR (L)

21
WATER
FLOW
CLEANSING
WAVE MECHANICS
LIFE FORCE
GROWTH
LEEK
SUBCONSCIOUS

ING (NG)

22
EARTH FATHER
POTENTIAL ENERGY
SATURDAY
GESTATION
COMPLETION OF BEGINNING

RUNIC STATES

DAGAZ (D, TH)

23
DAY
BREAKTHROUGH
POLARITY
VISIBLE SPECTRUM

OTHALA (O)

24
ANCESTRAL PROPERTY
SEPARATION
CLAN HOUSE
RETREAT
INBORN QUALITIES
FREEDOM
PROSPERITY
LEVERAGE PRINCIPLE

THE FAMILY GROUPING SYSTEM

The subconscious loves to pun around, use simile, use metaphor, and a symbol to stand for another object. As you use the runes, you will come to realize that a rune has a specific symbolic meaning for you, and that they fall into groups. You can then move them around, creating families that have meaning to you.

Since the runes are viewable on more than one plane at any time, it is exceedingly difficult to pin down a meaning in a reading. However, the runes can be grouped into families of runes with related meanings. Often these groups show up in readings and rune casts, acting as a sign post in how the rune should be read. This is a hint of how the subconscious is playing with the meanings, or substituting for unavailable runes.

There are two main reasons for doing this. Due to the multiple meanings, when you turn over a single rune, unless you have a very specific question, the many levels of symbolism in the rune can make the meaning of the answer unclear. When this occurs you normally must pull more runes to clarify the meaning. The additional runes may show a cause and effect or define a concept like a sentence, but sometimes no clear meaning unfolds. This is the time when studying the runes in family groups is valuable.

When you see a group's (or several groups') members in the seemingly unrelated jumble of runes that form the answer to a question; look for the common denominator to be primary to the answer of the question. When the answer rune is found in four groups, it is highly probable that the clarification runes will fall in one or two of the groups, or there will be other associated runes in the jumble.

The second reason is in the way your memory works. Recent studies show that the best analogy for your memory would be a peg board with paper clip chains stretching between the pegs similar to a string art picture. You remember a fact by hitting the peg that the paper clip fact is hooked to. In most cases the fact is in a chain of other sensory information or paper clips including emotions. The more chains a peg has, and the more pegs a clip is connected to, the easier it is to get to the information since you can start in any number of different pegs to get to the information.

Each rune becomes a fact like the paper clip in the chain of a family group. The reason for grouping is the peg the chain is hooked on. These pegs are such concepts as days of the week, fate, money, the clan, colors, and travel modes.

In management studies one of the first topics covered is Maslow's hierarchy of needs. Simply stated, the first needs to be met are food and shelter, then social acceptance and intellectual stimulus. In survival situations the needs are given up from last to first with the social interaction needs like recreation given up before respect and self-worth which are given up before shelter then food. Conversely, the more secure you are in your survival, the more your free time and list of "needs" grows.

In the tenth century food, as seen in FEHU - F, LAGUR - ſ, ELHAR - Y, and URUZ - ņ; and shelter, OTHALA - ⍟, BERKANO - ß, KENAZ - <, and THURISAR - ſ, were the prime concern of many people. Survival also meant having other people around to help in emergencies, such as your relations or clan, GEBO - X, and MANNAZ - M, WUNJO - ſ. After which there comes the runes of religious or spiritual matters NAUDHIR - ↓, TIWAR - ↑, ING - ◇, ANSUR - F, and HAEGEL - H.

Since we now have more free time to devote to pleasures and non-essential needs, we have a wider variety of groupings for the runes including one created to cover the energy and power concepts of quantum mechanics. As you work with the runes they will form groupings that hang on the pegs of your memory, and occasionally they will seem to shift and jump from peg to peg. This is normally due to shifts in the focus of your attention, what you deem most important in your life at the time, at what level of need you are operating from.

As you learn new information you can either add chains, pegs, or links in an existing chain. Many times you add a combination of all three. If the new information forces a redefinition of previous information the chains can slip off existing pegs to a new peg, or it may cause chains to merge. If closely related to an existing chain, it may only add a link or two to the existing chain, or add a branch in the chain.

The first family I want to discuss is that of the initiatory cycle, or cycle of life that Ralph Blum sets forth in his books. Dealing from a strictly Christian perspective as a mean to find what is happening in your life he arranges them in the following order with associated meanings.

INITIATIONS

FEHU - ᚠ	BECKONING
OTHALA - ᛟ	SEPARATION
URUZ - ᚢ	PATTERN TO COME
PERTHO - ᛈ	ŌRLOG
NAUDHIR - ᚾ	NEED
ING - ⋄	GESTATION
KENAZ - ᚲ	OPENING
BERKANO - ᛒ	BIRTH CYCLE/GROWTH
EHWAR - ᛗ	MOVEMENT/TRANSITION
HAEGEL - ᚺ	DISRUPTION
RAIDHO - ᚱ	JOURNEY
THURISAR - ᚦ	GATEWAY
DAGAZ - ᛞ	BREAKTHROUGH

Working from my experiences, very few cycles are seen like this. In my experience, there are stages that are extremely long and which overlap the next stage. In other instances there may seem to be a gap where nothing is occurring at all, a time of waiting and anticipation. So I modified and renamed the cycle as follows:

LIFE CYCLE

HAEGEL - ᚺ	DISRUPTION
KENAZ - ᚲ	OPENING
NAUDHIR - ᚾ	NEED

In this first section, the life cycle starts with a disruption in your life that awakens you to a need for a change. You become dissatisfied with the status quo. You feel a break with the old ways. Teenagers are a good example.

Between the parts of the cycle, there are very often breaks in activity where nothing seems to be happening. It will sometimes be true that nothing is happening there, but often it is more a case of waiting for the right time.

FEHU - ᚠ	PRAYER
ING - ⋄	GESTATION
URUZ - ᚢ	PATTERN TO COME
PERTHO - ᛈ	ŌRLOG

The second stage is where you break down and pray for guidance, or you have identified what it is that is making you unhappy, so you actively look for something better. There is a lot of waiting or gestation built into this stage itself. Eventually you have an idea of where you want to go, you just don't know how you are going to get there. As the old saying goes: *Running away gets you nowhere unless you have a firm destination in mind.*

ANSUR - F	INSPIRATION
OTHALA - ⋩	SEPARATION
EHWAR - M	TRANSITION
RAIDHO - R	JOURNEY
BERKANO - B	GROWTH
DAGAZ - M	BREAKTHROUGH

The third and last stage is where your prayer is answered and you see what you are to do. You know where you want to go, and you have an idea of how to get there. Then you have to do the physical work to bring your new reality about. The problem is then to break your old habits, start new ones, and allow them to grow until you finally reach your goal and make the breakthrough you were looking for. That is what the entire life cycle is all about, changing your reality to suit your spiritual growth.

The second family is that of physical matter.

MATTER

ISA - I	PRIMAL MATTER
URUZ - n	PATTERN OF MATTER TO COME

The family of success only has two members:

SUCCESS

TIWAR - ↑	VICTORY THROUGH SACRIFICE
SOWHILO - ϟ	SUCCESS

The astral travel family is similar in having only two members also:

ASTRAL

ELHAR - Y	SILVER CORD
MANNAZ - M	HEIMDALL, THE GUARDIAN, AND THE BRIDGE BRIFROST

There are two runes used for harmonious binding, such as when designing a bind rune. Though not very well suited, sometimes EHWAR - M and

ISA - I are added as a third and fourth member. Some add EHWAR - M because of marriage joining two people, but with the number of divorces, how good are most marriages? A marriage does not make two into one, each has to work at it still. An ice or cold weld will hold two items together until the stress gets great, then they both go their own way, so it too is really inappropriate here.

BINDING
WUNJO - ᚹ	HARMONY
GEBO - X	MANY IN ONE
EHWAR - M	MARRIAGE
ISA - I	STILLNESS

If you are interested in astrological correspondences, the grouping of runes with their planetary attachments may be useful.

PLANETS
WYRD -	MOON
SOWHILO - ᛋ	SUN
EIHWAR - ᛃ	MERCURY
KENAZ - <	VENUS
BERKANO - ᛒ	EARTH OR GAIA
TIWAR - ↑	MARS
THURISAR - ᚦ	JUPITER
ING - ◊	SATURN
PERTHO - ᛈ	URANUS
ANSUR - ᚠ	NEPTUNE
ISA - I	PLUTO

We find three members in the group related to money.

MONEY
OTHALA - ᛉ	PROSPERITY
FEHU - ᚠ	POSSESSIONS
URUZ - ᚾ	OXEN

Regeneration, like that performed by the Phoenix is found in a family with two members.

REGENERATION
KENAZ - <	DEATH AND SACRIFICE
SOWHILO - ᛋ	REGENERATION

RUNIC STATES

Fate and Fortune were important to those of the north, but were not something to be counted on. A minor accident could result in death or disaster.

FATE
PERTHO - ⌐	ORLOG (LAWS)
NAUDHIR - ✝	POWER OR NEED
WYRD -	DESTINY

We have three members in the family of light to see by:

LIGHT
DAGAZ - ⋈	DAY
SOWHILO - ϟ	LIGHTNING
WYRD -	DARKNESS

In the family of mankind and the clan there are three runes to describe these vital relations.

CLAN
MANNAZ - ᛘ	BLOOD BROTHER
WUNJO - ᚱ	BANNER
OTHALA - ⋆	HOUSE, LANDS

The functions of reproduction and sexuality is found in a family that was vital to the existence of the Clan.

SEXUALITY
GEBO - X	PLATONIC LOVE
KENAZ - <	FREYA (PASSION)
JERA - ᛡ	FREYR (FERTILITY)
EHWAR - ᛖ	SENSUALITY, FERTILITY

There are many deities associated with the runes as I explained in the previous text, though only a few close ties. These mostly balance in the Norse pantheon family of runes. The last two may require a little explanation. In the early times, Odhin, Loki, and Thor traveled about Midgaard a lot. Odhin and Loki became blood brothers, while Loki and Thor were close friends. Later, like many ex-friends, Loki and Thor became the bitterest of enemies as Loki directed many of his cruelest pranks at Thor, or his wife, Sif the fair.

DEITY
BERKANO - ᛒ	EARTH MOTHER
ING - ᛜ	EARTH FATHER
KENAZ - ᚲ	FERTILITY (FREYA)
JERA - ᛄ	FERTILITY (FREYR)
ANSUR - ᚠ	LOKI
THURISAR - ᚦ	THOR

When we look at colors associated with various runes, it seems to be useless, but sometimes such a relationship does have meaning. In one reading ISA was a representation not of snow or ice, but of a white water rafting expedition.

COLORS
WYRD -	BLACK
ISA - ᛁ	WHITE
KENAZ - ᚲ	RED
EIHWAR - ᛇ	GREEN
SOWHILO - ᛋ	GOLD

I have a family that comes up frequently now as the free time of our culture allows it, that of the arts.

ART
KENAZ - ᚲ	CREATIVITY
RAIDHO - ᚱ	RHYTHM AND DANCE
ANSUR - ᚠ	SONG AND POETRY

Methods of travel have changed in the last 1000 years, but the family of travel still is important.

TRAVEL
ELHAR - ᛉ	PLANE (SWAN)
RAIDHO - ᚱ	CAR (WAGON)
NAUDHIR - ᚾ	SHIP (SHIP'S MAST)
EHWAR - ᛖ	FOOT (HORSE)

Following the symbolism for each day in order to make the runic connection was bothering me for a while. The connection of the deities to some runes finally forced my hand to make these choices.

DAYS

WYRD -	MONDAY
TIWAR - ᛏ	TUESDAY
EIHWAR - ᛇ	WEDNESDAY
THURISAR - ᚦ	THURSDAY
KENAZ - ᚲ	FRIDAY
ING - ᛜ	SATURDAY
SOWHILO - ᛋ	SUNDAY

A family of spiritual runes has three basic members, though others are distant relations. Like some distant cousins, they show up at family reunions, but have little to do with the daily activities of the family. The most notable of these is EIHWAR - ᛇ.

SPIRIT

RAIDHO - ᚱ	DEVELOPMENT
ANSUR - ᚨ	POWER, KNOWLEDGE
TIWAR - ᛏ	DISCIPLINE

The family of time is sometimes is encountered in a reading, but is very hard to distinguish unless a time frame is specifically asked for.

TIME

JERA - ᛃ	YEAR
WYRD -	MONTH
DAGAZ - ᛞ	DAY

Life is a family with four members.

LIFE

BERKANO - ᛒ	LIFE CYCLE
LAGUR - ᛚ	LIFE FORCE
EIHWAR - ᛇ	SUSTAINER
ELHAR - ᛉ	HEALTH

There are many runes that came to have protective connotations. After all, it is a dangerous world out there, and in many instances it was best to hedge your bets.

PROTECTION
BERKANO - ᛒ	CONCEALMENT
HAEGEL - ᚺ	BANISHMENT
EIHWAR - ᛇ	DEFENSE
ELHAR - ᛉ	SANCTUARY
OTHALA - ᛟ	RETREAT
THURISAR - ᚦ	THORNS

There are only three members in the group for the forms of water.

WATER
ISA - ᛁ	ICE
HAEGEL - ᚺ	HAIL
LAGUR - ᛚ	FLOWING WATER

Magic is afoot in a runic family with esoteric discipline connections.

MAGIC
SOWHILO - ᛋ	MAGICAL WILL
PERTHO - ᛈ	SYNCHRONICITY
ELHAR - ᛉ	ASTRAL TRAVEL
JERA - ᛃ	KARMA

The items that man makes create a family of their own.

MAN-CRAFTED
THURISAR - ᚦ	HAMMER (MJOLLNIR)
SOWHILO - ᛋ	WHEEL
OTHALA - ᛟ	HOUSE
WUNJO - ᚹ	BANNER
PERTHO - ᛈ	DICE CUP
KENAZ - ᚲ	TORCH
RAIDHO - ᚱ	WAGON
NAUDHIR - ᚾ	SHIPS

In creating the bind rune for healing, I had to search for all of the runes that contained properties that are useful in healing. As a separate family, these would appear as follows:

HEALING

BERKANO - ᛒ	LIFE
LAGUR - ᛚ	CLEANSING FLOW
FEHU - ᚠ	CREATOR'S ENERGY
ANSUR - ᚨ	GROUNDING FLOW TO INJURY

The last family I will discuss now concern the energies and powers of traditional and quantum physics.

Energy is a difference in potential, force(s) provides the potential, and power is the potential applied to do work. Science only recognizes four forces at this time: electromagnetic, gravity, strong nuclear force, and weak nuclear force. The electromagnetic force is what everyone seems to want to divide into parts. Most of the time these pseudo-energies are called radiant energy (light), heat, and electrical.

First, let's examine the basic forces now recognized. Everyone should recognize gravity. It makes things fall down on earth. More universally, it is an attraction between two or more bodies based on their mass and the distance between them. The more physical particles such as atoms, an object has the greater the mass. The electromagnetic force is a wide spectrum of wavelengths released when electrons jump their shell, either freed from the atom altogether, or which then fall to a lower orbit or shell. The strong nuclear force refers to the bond between the parts of the atom's center or nucleus which keeps the nucleus together, while the weak nuclear force refers to force of radioactive nuclear decay which causes the nucleus to change to lighter and more stable forms. When you get down to basics, force is measured by the acceleration it can give a specific mass. In other words, force puts objects into motion, even if the objects are only small parts of atoms.

In many cases energy is typified by the way the potential of force is being stored. It can be stored in electricity, mechanical devices, chemicals, pressurized containers or any number of different manners. Einstein proved that the potential energy of any body was the mass of the body multiplied by the speed of light squared. In most cases that is a small number multiplied by a very large number. To put it in terms most people can relate to, the diamond from a normal engagement ring, usually less than one carat in weight, converted to its full potential energy and applied to moving a standard compact automobile, about one ton or 2,000 pounds, that is using it as pure power, the stone from that ring could move the automobile from the Earth to the nearest star other than our sun in about two years.

Power is the application of energy to produce movement or work, and is classified by the way it converts the energy to motion. Examples are hydroelectric, nuclear, and wind power generation systems. In practical terms, applying the energy to movement, becoming power, there is a tremendous amount of wasted energy. In the normal combustion engine in a car, a half carat weight of gas may fire one piston - once - getting you nowhere. If that amount of plutonium were used in a "hot" reactor in a car (one that is already at its operating temperature), it may get a hundred miles. In a "cold" reactor it would be lucky to get around the block. In both examples, so much energy is lost in wasted heat and remains locked in physical mass that most of the potential energy stored is never tapped.

This does not take into account the forces and energies that the scientists cannot measure with their machines or understand well enough to describe mathematically. Einstein never finished the unified field theory tying gravity to electromagnetism. The mathematical symbols he needed did not exist at that time. Once his theory is finished it may also tie in life forces and energies such as pyramid and orgone energies. This could also give the proofs and explanations needed for such things as telepathy, psychokinesis, and precognition. All these are things that science relegates to the fringes and unexplained mass hysteria.

In order to study the connections of the runes to the quantum mechanics, we must remember the definitions of force, energy, and power as used by said quantum mechanics. We must also make certain we abide by the conventions and not be sloppy in our use, or the relations of runes to concepts will be useless.

POWER

ISA - I	INERTIA
FEHU - F	PRIMAL EXPANSION
URUZ - n	PATTERN'S FORCE
LAGUR - r	LIFE FORCE
KENAZ - <	SUB-ATOMIC BONDING FORCE
ING - ◊	POTENTIAL ENERGY
THURISAR - ▶	KINETIC ENERGY
RAIDHO - R	MECHANICAL ENERGY
NAUDHIR - ✻	FATES' POWER
HAEGEL - H	ELEMENTAL POWER
SOWHILO - ϟ	ELECTRICITY

RUNIC STATES

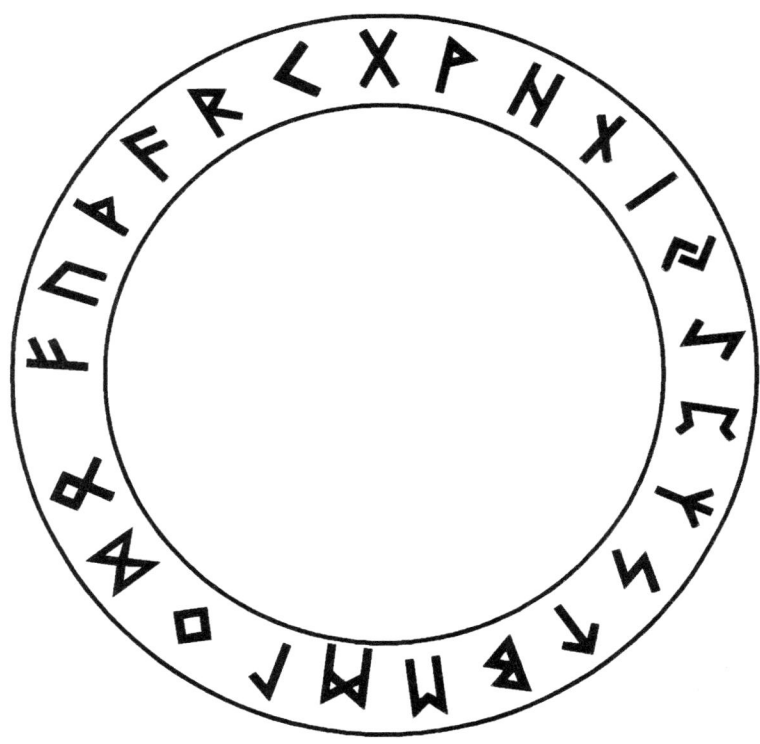

Chapter 5: RUNIC TOOLS

RUNE FLASHCARDS

The first step I took when I seriously started to study the runes was to make a set of flashcards. Using standard three by five cards I placed the rune on one side with name, sound, and associated number on the other side. Later I added the various meanings of the rune on the side with the name.

Like crystals growing out of a solution, the more you work with symbols, the more they tend to bump together and fit together like pieces of a giant jigsaw puzzle. As I worked with the flashcards I began to notice multiple connections between the runes. I sat down one evening and charted these connections. The runes had divided themselves into 22 groups or families.

Eventually, I began to do readings for others where I would see these groups appearing. Like some languages, the runes could be described as having male, female, and neuter genders. Each rune could be read on a mental, a physical, and a spiritual level as well as having a sound, a shape, and a number. Since there are multiple meanings or levels for each rune, each rune can be found in more than one group or family.

RUNE SET

The rune set I use consists of one inch square red oak tiles with all 24 of the standard Elder Futhark which is the set of runes I have described here, plus the blank WYRD -   tile is represented. The tiles are stored in a velvet bag when not in use.

The runes are hand carved on the oak tiles. Red enamel is used to fill the carvings. The tiles are then oiled with furniture grade lemon oil as a preservative and to purify the rune set. The tiles are oiled once or twice a year.

The use of the rune set in meditation and divinatory rune readings is fairly easy and straight forward since each tile has only one rune on it, and can be drawn individually. After being drawn from the bag, the tile can be used alone for meditation or placed in a layout for interpretation as a runecast. This process is described in the next chapter.

RUNE BOARD

Before the advent of the printing press made books readily available, learning to read was frequently accomplished off of a sampler. The sampler was usually stitched by a mother or sister with the alphabet and a saying sewn onto it; a "sample" of sewing skill using various techniques, and a pattern for learning the alphabet.

There have been many articles found with the runes carved on them, several which could be described as rune boards or runic wands. Some, such as the piece of whalebone found when an ancient tavern was being torn down, had the runes carved on all sides, while others had them only on one side. There is even the case of the Futhark, or runic alphabet, being carved on a column in a church.

Some of the artifacts having all the runes carved once on one side could be considered a rune board. The rune board, and its larger version the rune table, can be used as a device for meditation, a portable altar, or as a divination tool.

The rune boards I make are a smoothed plank of hardwood about twelve inches long and six inches wide. After carving, the runes are filled with red enamel, the entire piece is given a final sanding, and then oiled with a furniture grade lemon oil. A more traditional oil would be linseed oil which is an empowering oil, but lemon oil is both purifying and protective.

In using the board as a meditation device, or as a sampler, sit with the board in your lap, place yourself in a receptive state of mind, and then place a finger on the rune you wish to study. Alternatively, you may simply gaze on the rune you wish to meditate on. An understanding or a new view of the rune normally comes to me with this technique.

I place a candle on the Wyrd rune that is in the center of the rune board when I use it as an altar. You may also place a taper or candle on one of the runes if you wish to empower the rune or draw it into your life. If you consider an altar as a place to hold your implements while working magic, then a rune board can be a sanctified place from which to work while traveling.

In divination, the rune board's use is similar to that while using it for meditation, except after placing the board in your lap and clearing your mind, you concentrate on a question. As you run your fingers over the runes on the board, you may find one which feels sticky or holds your fingers. In any case you should find one which feels different, this is the one that is your answer.

RUNE TABLE

The uses of the rune board and rune table are basically the same with two major differences. First the rune table is much larger than the rune board, the size will vary, but it is about the same size as a coffee table, so it is not very portable. Second, the rune table is intended for use as a runic altar, and as such is very personal. Each one is created and is personalized with the name of the person, be it magical, mundane, or a medicine name, along with an affirmation or prayer chosen by the person. These are both set in runes carved into the bottom or rails of the table.

The carvings of the name and affirmation set into the table are not filled with enamel or specifically empowered so they do not overpower the filled runes on the top of the table. As a symbol, each rune holds its own power, yet the power of an affirmation or name is greater than that of a single rune. Synergy makes the sum greater than the parts, but even more, the power of your will in carving the affirmation and holding it to be set in the carving is what will multiply the effect of the affirmation. The carving alone does not have a tenth of the power that the will can infuse in it.

BIND RUNES

Basically a bind rune is created to make a new rune with more meanings out of simple single runes. Edred Thorsson covers the magical and mystical rules for creating a bind rune out of several giving due consideration for numerology of the runes used and the purpose of the bind rune. In both ceremonial and high magic many of the props, gestures, and symbols are carefully constructed with thought given to the impact of numerical and astrological correspondence. However, the shaman, or healer, or low magic practitioner deal more with a feeling of rightness or the overall fit into the pattern being created. The rules are elemental (pun intended) rather than numerical. It is more of a question of "Is this sentence pleasing to the ear and effective?" than "Does this fall in the proper poetic meter for the result?" When imagery is important, simple is sometimes more effective. It is for this reason that I look at the meanings and forms of the runes, not bothering as much with the numerical value assigned to the runes in creating a bind rune. Besides, various authors and authorities place the runes in different orders, assigning different values to the runes.

When I say that the shaman is more concerned with the elemental properties of a plant, or in this discussion a rune, rather than a number, this is not to say a simple is simple. When dealing with herbs, a simple is a preparation of a single plant or mineral with appropriate properties, just like dealing with a single rune. When multiple herbs are blended together, or a bind rune created, the elemental property of the plants are given careful thought. For example: lung problems always concern the air element, but a congestion could be a water element while burning bronchitis sensation a fire element condition. The shaman or herbalist decides whether to use opposites to fight, or like to reduce gently the symptoms, and the preparation fixed accordingly. If we assume the decision is to cool the fire with water, the plants will combine the elements of air and water to fight the fire of bronchitis, no plants with a fire element will be used. To do so could nullify the effectiveness of the preparation and possibly aggravate the condition. Thus a bind rune would not likely combine LAGUR - ſ, water, and KENAZ - <, fire, unless steam was wanted or I would be dealing with just an alphabetical use for the runes.

Before covering the bind rune as a name, I will cover the four standard bind runes I created for meditations and prayers by anyone. All of these are on approximately three inch by four inch walnut plaques. I have made the medicine tree bind rune on exotic, resinous wood by special request.

The first bind rune is UNITY. This bind rune has a basic makeup of BERKANO - ᛒ and ING - ◊, the Earth mother and Earth father runes. As such it represents the greater unity possible in duality; where you cannot differentiate one without contrasting it to the other. In it can be found sixteen of the twenty-five elder runes. As a study in polarity and duality this bind rune is helpful in finding and maintaining balance in life.

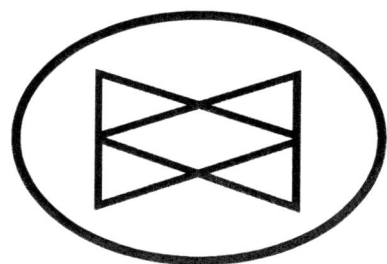

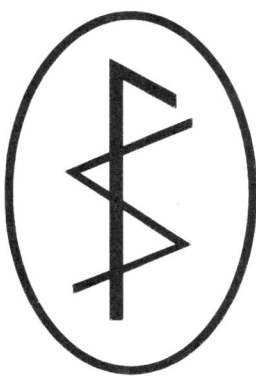

The second bind rune is PROSPERITY. This bind rune consists of SOWHILO - ᛋ and LAGUR - ᛚ, a field of success, and growth. Results of the sun and water nurturing plants to grow, prosperity in farming. In American culture they form the dollar sign, the definitive form of prosperity. Viewed as a bind rune, the natural gifts of sunshine and water allow the plants to prosper for our benefit, perhaps even a money tree growing in your life.

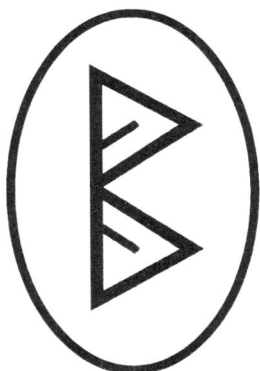

The third bind rune is called HEALING. There are four runes combined to form this bind rune: BERKANO - ᛒ, LAGUR - ᛚ, FEHU - ᚠ, and ANSUR - ᚠ. LAGUR - ᛚ and FEHU - ᚠ facilitate the flow of new energy to clear out blockages and any negative energy, including ensuring a good blood supply to the region. The second group of FEHU - ᚠ and ANSUR - ᚠ are the prayer and blessing, requesting a healing and acknowledging its coming. Finally, these are bound within the Birch tree and Earth Goddess, BERKANO - ᛒ, to promote growth beyond the status quo.

An injury requires flow around it. Blood flow for new cell growth, and an energy flow slightly above normal for/from the increased cell activity. After placing FEHU - ᚠ and LAGUR - ᛚ with BERKANO - ᛒ I noticed that not only are the two types of flow there, but the two aspects of prayer as well. I intentionally placed FEHU - ᚠ there as a prayer for healing and found that ANSUR - ᚨ, the receipt of the blessing of a prayer was also formed.

With the balance achieved for the Healing bind rune, I looked to see what other runes were hidden in it. ISA - ᛁ, the straight line of stillness is there joining the five major runes as is WUNJO - ᚹ, a binding rune of harmony and new energy. SOWHILO - ᛋ, the sun or regeneration is found. So are RAIDHO - ᚱ, spiritual development, and KENAZ - ᚲ for regeneration are also there. These extra runes as well as LAGUR - ᛚ above are all found in the shape of BERKANO - ᛒ. So BERKANO - ᛒ by itself could be used for healing, the only things my additions added that was not there before are the energy flow and receipt of prayer and resulting blessings.

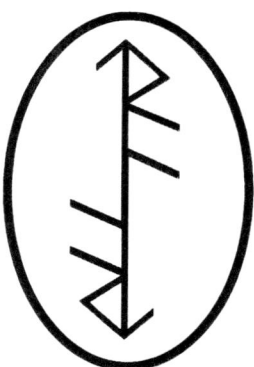

The final standard bind rune is the MEDICINE TREE. This bind rune has the properties of LAGUR - ᛚ, RAIDHO - ᚱ, TIWAR - ᛏ, and ANSUR - ᚨ bound on EIHWAR - ᛇ. This is spiritual power, development, knowledge, and discipline attached to the world tree with life. Spiritual advancement through life's worldly challenges. The likeness to the native American spears and their concept of medicine power merge well with Odhin's wisdom and power acquired hanging on the Yew tree.

The story of how I created the medicine tree bind rune is a good example of how a shaman forms a bind rune. During a medicine trip meditation I was met by one of my power animals, a bird. As we flew it turned into a

Raven, not it's normal form. We flew up a cliff to a stand of yew trees on the top where the wind blowing the limbs made them look like feathers on a spear. I was to remember this and the meditation ended.

A raven is a bird of portent and the familiar of Odhin, providing him with tales of all that occurs, much as the native American consider it a bird with much knowledge. A few weeks later I was moved to make a bind rune for a person named Raven, the victim of religious persecution. As I worked with the runes to spell Raven, I realized that almost all of the runes dealing with spiritual development were there, and the memory of the medicine trip surfaced.

I was compelled to change what I was planning on doing and create the medicine tree bind rune. The form was to be similar to the feather decorated spears of the Native Americans as the trees of the medicine dream indicated. Three different forms were considered, but the feel was better for the one chosen.

As a test, I tried a meditation with the bind rune I had carved. The meditation turned into a normal trip to the upper spirit world starting out. However, instead of landing in the land of the clouds, I landed on a rainbow bridge with a large guy blocking the way. When he saw the bind rune I carried, he let me pass.

About then I realized I was on Brifrost, passed Heimdall, and was on my way to Asgaard. By the time I arrived, it was almost time for my return. I had accomplished what I set out to do, prove that I had chosen the right bind rune form.

Having returned, I questioned how my meditation was able to get me to Asgaard, past the guardian of the bridge. I could only make a twofold guess. First, this bind rune is a symbol for spiritual development, and I was on a proper shaman's journey. Second, the raven is the familiar of Odhin, and the bind rune is the form of the spirit raven. In a way, I became a messenger like Huginn and Muninn, Odhin's raven familiars.

This brings up the last form of a bind rune I will cover, a name set in a bind rune. The following shows two major forms for doing a name as a bind rune, either on a line, or joined by GEBO - X, a "binding" rune which harmonizes the forces of the runes on it.

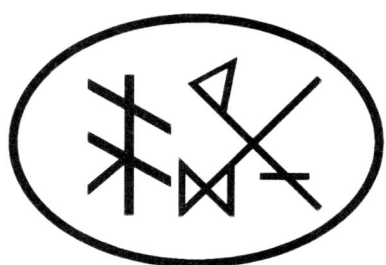

The straight line bind rune is NIT (Night) as represented by NAUDHIR - ↛, ISA - I, and TIWAR - ↑. The spelling of the name Night is modified to be more phonetic and double letters are represented by a single rune. The GEBO - X bound rune is WIND as shown by WUNJO - ⌐, ISA - I, NAUDHIR - ↛, and DAGAZ - ⋈. The second rune for Wind is the easiest of the two, a straight phonetic substitution of runes for letters placed on GEBO - X.

In this bind rune for NIT WIND, look at the Tiwar rune at the bottom of the straight line. There is the extra upward slanting line on the left which makes the bottom section look like a combination of NAUDHIR - ↛ and TIWAR - ↑ instead of ISA - I and TIWAR - ↑.

Remember, spelling is subject to change and language has evolved since the runes were in use as the alphabet. I started this bind rune on the straight line of ISA - I, at the top placing NAUDHIR - ↛, need. The stillness and ego of ISA - I is the base holding need above and victory in TIWAR - ↑ below. However, still in the "i" sound we have another rune EIHWAR - ↕, the Yew tree, being EI, the long "i". So I added the upward slant on the left.

This gives a bit more meaning to the bind rune without changing the pronunciation. EIHWAR - ↕ is a rune of communication, bringing heaven's gifts to us, and carrying our prayers upward. In this bind rune, EIHWAR - ↕ is rooted in NAUDHIR - ↛ above and NAUDHIR - ↛ below. In addition, it adjoins but does not take part in TIWAR - ↑, victory in the earth plane. Its influence is passed through NAUDHIR - ↛ below to TIWAR - ↑ below on the plane formed by ISA - I.

Metaphysically, this gives the dark and cool night where dreams and needs are often expressed and sometimes fulfilled. That time where the minds of men turn to the stars and the questions of those things larger than themselves, and the time when the younger couples turn to love watching the moon. Power, matter, need and success are joined into a single form.

RUNE WAND

The wand is an article used to project and receive energies for manipulation. With the Rune Board, the energies of the runes were mainly used in meditation and divination, but with a taper or a candle, the energy of a particular rune was brought out for use. With the Rune Wand, the runes are carved on more than one side of the wand, normally a square piece of wood about twelve inches long.

The layout of the runes on the wand is different for each wand. The placement of the runes on the wand is determined by the use the wand is wanted for. If the wand is for projection of energy, projective runes are around the tip, and what is desired to be projected close behind. The runes of power sources are placed behind that of the energy to be projected, in the place where a projective finger can be placed on it. If carved for a right hand, the runes are in a different place than for a left hand.

Now to discuss the reasoning behind the rune wand's difference. In the studies of oriental chi or life force, the force is said to run in meridians or channels down the torso, arms, and legs. Traditional western esoteric studies agree in many respects including receptive and projective hands and fingers, as in the Yin and Yang meridians in the hands and fingers. In general, your dominant hand is projective, normally the right but sometimes the left hand, while the other hand is receptive. With the fingers it is even more confusing.

The receptive/projective question in relation to the fingers is a bit tough. Traditional lore has two of each meridian type on each hand with the thumb being a little of neither and a little of both. Kirlian photography of some people show projective index and ring fingers while on a yogi all fingers and thumb projected equally. The dominant hand has stronger projecting meridians while the other hand has stronger receptive meridians.

The wand is used like a flute with the projective finger placed on a rune to be empowered for projection. If the wand is for a reception, a receptive finger is place on the receptive rune to be empowered. Use the thumb as a ground or as a moderator instead of an activator. Place one thumb (or both of them since you can use both hands) on a rune of lesser importance to your purpose.

In my case, I am almost ambidextrous and may have swapped channels to have the projective and receptive meridians grouped instead of alternating fingers. My personal feeling is projective index and middle fingers with the ring and little finger being receptive on the right hand. In the fingers of the left hand there is very little difference between being receptive or projective. This is a matter for you to test and learn for yourself. Are you left handed? Do you have some fingers that are more sensitive or feel warmer on the color red or cooler on the color blue? Or do they work in the reverse? These are excellent clues as to whether the finger is receptive or projective.

In the more recent research into shamanism, there was information on varying the wand's length to match certain wavelengths, like those put out by the brain in various activities like meditating and sleeping. The theory said the material in the wand did not matter as much as matching the wavelength which is close to the return to the basics of radio.

In the early days of crystal radio sets, the reception the crystal in the set had to be matched to the length of your antenna. You could use 1/2 of a wavelength, a full wavelength, or multiple wavelengths for the antenna. Minor tuning between wavelengths would be accomplished with the crystal and circuits in the radio.

Working with these premises, I was able to confirm a few theories, and identify some of the principles:

1) Wavelength is critical.
2) Material does not matter.
3) Lengths of wands are cumulative when joined at the ends.
4) Crystals round and tune between wavelengths.
5) Use of ferrous or metallic materials requires polishing or capping the ends to allow for wave reflection.

What I found was the length for the wands was critical, so critical in fact that as little as 1/8 of an inch or one millimeter could have dramatic and discernable differences in feel. When the right length is found, the wand acts as an antenna, pulling in the power for the wand, storing it, and sending it out again.

While working on the wands, I found the length that produces at least a magnitude of difference in feeling by sanding a bit off, testing it, and sanding more. I started with a length several of the references had recommended plus a half inch. At that length it was still a dead piece of carved wood. As I turned the secondary end, I made frequent stops to test the feel of the wand. By the time I got within an eighth of an inch of my target length I began to get a feedback feeling.

I shaped the primary end, and continued to shorten it to the recommended target length. In the end, I found the feeling peaked at one millimeter less than the theoretical length.

RUNIC STATES

Chapter 6: TECHNIQUES

CARVING RUNES

When I carved my first rune set I tried the techniques Edred Thorsson described in *FUTHARK*. A knife is used to create a flat surface, then a ristir is used to carve the rune, and finally it is colored in with a triangular object. The results were less than satisfactory. Looking at the pictures of the tools suggested their common names: kitchen knife, awl, wood brush.

If you examine the objects and crafts from the time of the runes, everything from 200 ce to 1100 ce, they were much more sophisticated than Edred Thorsson gave them credit for. Since the runes where worked predominately in wood, and I was going to be working in wood, I chose to use traditional carpentry tools of the periods. If I chose to work in metal, I might have picked a metal engraver similar to the awl Edred Thorsson suggested, or even some steel chisels or stamps. You can go to almost any good wood specialty store and find fine carving knives and hand chisels whose form has remained unchanged for over 2000 years. The local hardware store may have a cheaper set of knives available made of soft iron from the pacific rim nations.

Over ninety percent of the carving I do is done with either a quarter inch or two centimeter straight chisel point carving knife. The other chisel point that I commonly use is one half the size of the first that I use for carving the smaller lines in the shape of ING - ◊ and OTHALA - ᛟ. Occasionally, the grain of a piece of wood requires a forty-five degree angle point knife to clean up excess wood in the carving, or to put an clean end on a long cut. A file and a dressing stone are used to keep the tools sharp.

An ordinary paint brush or reed can be used to apply the pigment to the runes. Paint brushes have been made of hair for more than 3000 years. An alternative is to crush the end of a reed or stem of a plant to produce a brush.

The pigments used to fill the runes carved are traditionally red. I use the red lacquer sold for painting models in filling the runes I carve. All civilizations in history considered red to be an empowering color, and most had access to ocher for the pigment. There are some tales of a drop of blood being rubbed into the carving to empower the rune. Some sources state that sealing the blood in a carving with pine pitch, resin, or a pine based lacquer seals you to the rune, making it impossible to avoid troublesome calls.

The first carving done with the carving knives was a wand for an acquaintance. As I sat on the steps of the house carving the runes onto the wand I had a flash of a vision. I sat on a sunny hillside carving the runes into a panel for decorating a piece of furniture. The forest was beautiful with evergreens all the way down into the blue gray waters of the fjord. The tools I had for the carving was a set of carving knives and chisels with handles different than the ones I used while sitting on my steps, but similar points. Definitely not empirical proof of my theory, but subjective substantiation if you want to consider reincarnation.

The last point in considering a carving of a runic tool is how are you going to finish the hardwood surface. From the first, I was adverse to applying a lacquer or finish over the carvings. I chose to use lemon oil to finish the pieces I carved. Lemon is not a traditional oil for use in the far northern reaches of Europe. Citrus trees do not grow there. A traditional oil would be Linseed oil from the flax plant which is used to magically empower items.

Lemon has three properties which make it more useful for my purposes. First, the oil protects the wood the item is made of. Second, the oil has a slight empowering effect. Not as strong as Linseed oil, it still empowers the runes carved, and the item the runes are carved in. Finally, lemon oil is a purifier and so will purify the article for use, removing some of the traces of the person who carved the article from it to make it more suitable for use.

THE RUNE READING

When you have your own rune set, you soon find there are many ways to perform a rune reading or rune cast. Even though it is called a rune cast, I do not recommend casting the tiles of the rune set for an answer to a question. When you draw a tile while concentrating on the question, you allow your superconscious to guide your hand to the tile for your answer. When you throw the tiles you reduce the answer to chance. That is why I prefer to call it a rune reading instead of a rune cast in all but one instance.

Let's start with the simplest rune reading, a single tile draw. When you focus on a question or topic, then draw a tile, that is your answer to meditate on. You have just done a single tile draw.

The next layout is a line draw where three tiles are pulled to answer the question. The normal interpretation of these are cause, course of action, and outcome, though that can change depending on the question. This is close to a past, present, and future reading.

Basically any layout from any form of divination can be used with the runes since the runes are the symbols you are working with to define your question and answer. This includes such intricate draws as a Celtic Tarot layout, even though you only have twenty-five tiles to use in the runes. One person who did a reading for me had me draw nine tiles, three lines of three tiles, then threw out the lines that did not feel right. Another person I know uses a short layout form from the Tarot. The layout is the format of the answers the symbols lie in.

There is one important feature of using the runes for divination that is easily overlooked. Divination is use of symbols and intuition or psychic ability to divine the will of the divine. Whether the divine will is of your deity or super conscious, your subconscious is the interpreter for the reading, and it enjoys punning around with the symbols you use. When the divine causes you to pull out a rune, it may not be the exact, best fit symbol for your answer, especially since it is probably a multiple draw layout. By this I mean the first rune you draw should be the best fit for that question and that position in the layout. The rest of the positions cannot use that rune again, and so must make do with the next closest rune.

There are two ways to get around this problem of not having multiple copies of one rune. First, you could write down the rune drawn and place it back in the pile to be used again if needed. The second way is to start your drawing for the positions in the layout that are central to the question being read for, and work out to the less critical positions. Finally, there is a work around that is built into the symbolism of the runes, that were multiple runes have similar but slightly varying meanings.

The format I normally use for a reading is a three by three matrix with the first column being the past, the middle column being the present, and the right column being the future. The top row is the spiritual level, the middle row is the mental or astral plane, and the bottom is the row of the physical realm. This gives a reading with a varying duration; each column being anything from a couple of months to a couple of years in duration.

When a diagonal is formed in any of these layouts, they represent the "As above, so below" and the "As you sow, so you reap" axioms since you are either receiving the answers to your prayers, or sending things out for later return.

In the reading, the runes can appear upright, upside down, or on their side. The reversed rune is taken as a challenge condition existing or one of the more negative meanings associated with that particular rune. The upright appearance is read with the meaning for that particular level (physical, mental, or spiritual). A rune on its side is in transition, it may be moving from reversed to upright, or it may be one that is not quite in focus for the time period (past, present, future) being drawn.

As an example, RAIDHO - R in transition in the present could be a journey just completed, one in the near future, or one that may not be taken because of over riding circumstances. Depending on the runes drawn and the time feeling, the journey could have been almost in the past (1 plus months to 18 months) or almost future (1 plus month to 18 months) in any case, it is the most significant rune to the present condition that is not being used in some other position of the layout.

Now, when the person I am performing the rune reading for does not recognize the situation, or I am unsure as to what the meaning is, I do a supplemental reading to expand on the rune in question. To do this first lay the rune in question in the center of the work space. Then draw more tiles to lay around it in the form of the rune in question. Those runes below the question rune form the base of the problem, those above are contributing factors or outside influences, the left is past, and the right the future. This is very similar to the Tarot reading methods.

The grouping of runes with similar meanings are invaluable in identifying tracks or themes running through the reading. This can sometimes be a clue to unraveling a knotty reading, or show a slant not verbalized but desired in the answer. This can even override the normal position of the rune in the reading. For example, the rune shows on the physical level, but the other runes in that level form a group of the astral or spiritual meanings, not physical meanings. This would lead to the possibility that the person is primarily concerned with spiritual aspects of life.

There is one more historical way to do a rune *cast* for a venture or project oriented question. This is to use gaming sticks with selected runes on them as used in the Viking game. Only the three runes and fortune symbol are used. The two success runes are placed back to back to form one cylinder symbolizing success through your plans. The other two fortune symbols are back to back forming the second cylinder in your hand which symbolizes the forces of favorable and unfavorable fortune.

As you tap the cylinders down on a wood surface (traditionally ash or oak is preferred), concentrate on your project. Cast the sticks onto a hard surface and read the symbols which show. You will have some combination of unconditional success, victory through sacrifice or compromise, good fortune which is usually success, misfortune, and the blank backs which is a no comment answer.

WRITING WITH RUNES

It may seem that I keep repeating myself on one point. It does not matter what language you use when you work with the runes since the runes are symbols. As symbols they lie on the same level as the language in the psyche. The only differences the languages you know will make in using the runes is which thought patterns will be easier to use. Eventually, the runes will bring new thought patterns in their relations.

R. I. Page goes into the traditional writing styles using the runes. There are a few points that may seem strange at first. The inscriptions on most jewelry did not have the name of the person giving or receiving the gift, rather the inscription read "So-and-so made me", an early form of trade marks. Isn't that romantic? Many of the other inscriptions had magical connotations or invocations to various deities.

One last point needs to be covered in more detail. It all goes back to runes took quite a bit of time to cut, totally unlike the pen and paper we are used to. A sentence with thirty or forty runes could take a couple of hours to cut in wood, or over a day to cut in stone. Therefore many inscriptions found written in runic form are also done in a form of short hand.

The most common form is to eliminate unnecessary letters. These include all silent letters such as the final "e" and instances of double letters such as the double "t" in the word letter. When you encountered a double rune, it normally meant there was a word division there. One word ended in a rune and the next started with the same rune. The words in sentences could either run together or be separated by an extra space or be indicated by mirror imaging the runes in the new word. Many rune carvers seemed to prefer to run them together.

Another form of shorthand is to use a rune symbolically. An example would be to use KENAZ - < for the word torch. This would probably be used most often in reference to a deity, using ING - ◊ to refer not to the NG sound, but to the God Ing. This is very similar to the pictograph use of many cultures before writing began to represent individual sounds. This also accounts for the null or foreign symbols found in some runic works.

An example of intrusive non-runic symbols is found in a ring sent to me by the retired sea captain I worked with on Der Wikinger, the Viking game. His grandfather worked on the excavation of the Gokstadt ship in 1881. Found in a field near Vestfold, Norway, this Viking chieftain's funeral ship from some when around 900 ce The chieftain was only 5 foot tall, and the ring is proportionally small, about a size 4 or 5 in today's measurements. The ring I was sent is made from a cast of the original ring found with the chieftain.

This is a ring in the shape of the typical five pointed tiara type crown. Cast in a silver alloy, it appears to be a beautiful example of modern sand cast jewelry. This allowed the runes and rim of the ring to be raised relief with a beautiful texture around the runes. The runes are in a Norse dialect invoking the intercession of Vidar, one of the sons of Odhin who is given as the God of kings and other governors of large territories.

While most of the runes on the ring are standard elder FUTHARK runes, there are some foreign to this set. These could be a local dialect or a fashion of the craftsman making the ring. There are a few inverted and mirror imaged runes in the inscription which could be indications of word change. There is what appears to be a bind rune consisting of NAUDHIR - ↑, and LAGUR - ↾ or ANSUR - ⨍ on the ring as well. Under the points immediately to the right and left of the center point are two symbols totally foreign to the known rune sets which efface runes below them or which contain runes on their rim. The symbol on the left is a circle with two legs or runes beneath it. The symbol on the right is a stylized steer head covering three runes or having three legs beneath it.

This ring is a wonderful example of using the runes as a writing form. There are evidences of symbolic shorthand, dialect changes to the runes' form, and personal style and habit of the craftsman in use in the inscription on this ring. Also, this ring is a monument to the craftsmanship of the Vikings. This is no crude scratch and fill project, but the work of a master silversmith and would be the envy of many jewelers today.

RUNIC STATES

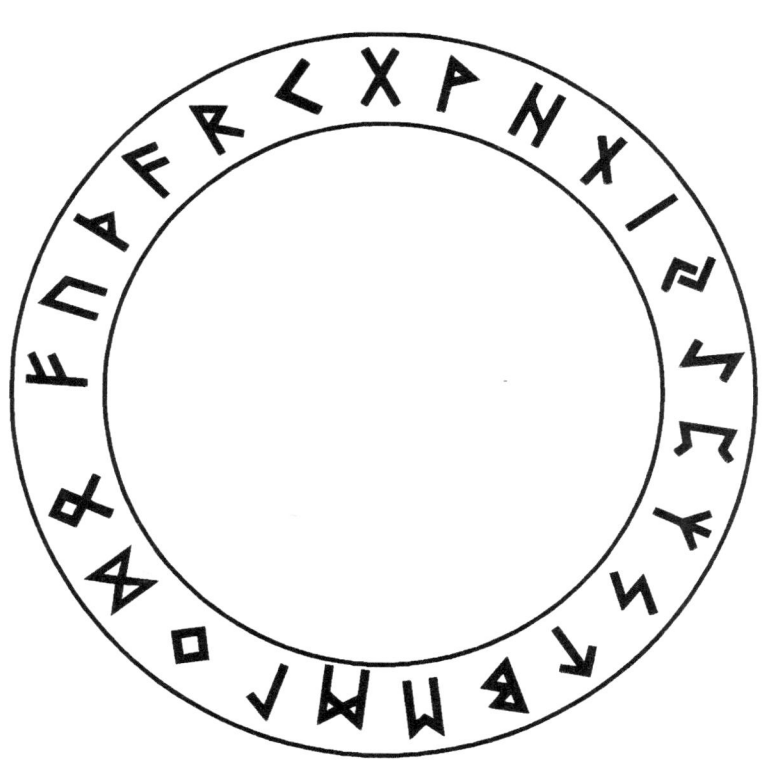

RUNIC STATES

Chapter 7: DER WIKINGER – (THE VIKINGS)

A HISTORIC RUNE GAME

This chapter is an example of the use of runes and other symbology as they were used almost 1200 years ago, and an example in how to analyze the symbology in the runes for your own use. I have been working with a German sea captain to recreate a runic game he played as a child. The original game boards were found in some archaeological excavations in the later part of the last century and early in the 1900s.

The title he gave to the game was "A Viking game: The journey through life to Valhalla". This is shortened to THE VIKINGS or Der Wikinger depending on the language you wish to use. The original boards found in the excavations were made of oak or ash. I made the prototype boards for the new game of ash as it is given as a the world tree in some of the myths, others give it as a yew tree.

The game is played similar in concept to Parchesi or Backgammon in that the players move the pieces along the board, setting opponents back, creating blockades, and the end comes when one player gets all his pieces off the board to home or in this case Valhalla.

It is very old Germanic culture in its concepts of play. It is possible to play with the pieces being ships or men, either the sea life of a Viking, or the home and hearth battles of the landsmen. Fate and fortune play major roles in the course of the game, for long periods of time it is possible to go nowhere until fortune intervenes, or fate leaves you alone.

There are special squares on the board representing for the sea going a ship repair yard, safe harbors, and a square of shoals or the shipwrecked's lamps. For the landsmen these squares are the clan hearth, forts, and ignominious defeat in battle. Both game versions have one square in common, the Edelweiss, a flower representing purity, and in this game, purification before the death which allows you to enter Valhalla.

Unlike the modern games, the players do not throw dice, but rather sticks with runes carved on them. The sticks can fall with the blank side up, representing no move, or a rune which allows one square movement. The runes used are SOWHILO - ↯, the sun or success; TIWAR - ↑, victory through self-sacrifice; HAEGEL - H, disruption or set backs brought on by FATE; and a symbol not really a rune, the Norse sun wheel, a symbol of good fortune. For all normal purposes each stick counts one point, with the exception of the sun wheel and HAEGEL - H, which have the special properties of being Fortune and Fate. Fate, HAEGEL - H, has a negative effect on all throws where it shows up unless Fortune, the sun wheel, intervenes to offset the negative one square of HAEGEL - H. But Fortune in appearance with the other two runes has no special powers.

This is very indicative of the feelings of many of the Northern Germanic Tribes. That being, they saw that the works of the Gods and Fate where normally to the detriment of the normal people. A man could make his own way and fortune, but then circumstances beyond his control would play havoc with his plans. On rare occurrence, the Gods or good Fortune would intervene, not to give aid as a reward, but rather to offset the ravages of Fate.

This is plainly evident in the stories and myths where Thor and the other Gods would aid people of Midgaard, usually only as a thorn to spoil the fun and depredations of the Giants. The rare times in exception were to the people that were to be mighty heroes or lords of the land and likely candidates for the halls of Valhalla. In other words, those aided were those likely to be an aid in the Gods' struggles at Ragnarok, the last battle against the Giants.

One more point here. The Germanic Tribes were one of the few early peoples who did not have extremely rigid caste type divisions between the classes. A man could work his way up the social ladder through his own merit. Most could make the step from free landsman or merchant to professional warrior, especially since there was little difference between them. All free men were subject to call by the lords to fight, and merchants were always under the hazard of attack for their goods. The main difference being that the professional warrior was excellent enough in skills of arms to win a place as a retainer for a lord, and often was rewarded with land of his own. The second step to the nobility and the leaders was possible to a fewer number but still possible.

Each level of the game is like that too, even though all pieces start off ranked as landsmen/merchants, the leaders reach warrior status earlier at the shipyard/clan land. When they reach the last rank of nobility, they are able to form blockades, and are subject to the perils of the shoals or ignominious defeat. Unlike the life of the Germanic tribes, all the pieces in the game pass through the last rank to reach Valhalla.

There are many correlations that one can draw from the game for today's life as well, for we still suffer the stones and arrows of misfortune. The young still are in last place, unable to make plans for themselves since the power lies with those aged, lucky, and crafty enough to seize what they want. Just look at all the rich politicians.

As I was working on the runes for the shipyard, the harbor, and the shoals because the meanings of the runes for the shoals and harbor did not quite tie in to the meanings of the runes as we know them from most sources. The Edelweiss for the last square was kept as the concept of death being a transition and an act of purification is represented by it.

For the shipyard, WUNJO - ᛒ is joy or the clan banner, and RAIDHO - ᚱ is a wagon. Together they represent the Werks where the clan smithy and wrights were located, where the wagons and ships could be built by the craftsmen. This is almost the exact reasoning used by the one of the archaeologists in studying the game board and a very good example in the way words and pictographs work. When a new word is called for in German, many times a whole new word is not created out of random or almost random letters (unlike *ADVIL, FRISBEE*, and many other products on the American store shelves), but rather two or more words to describe the article are joined like a sentence fragment. English sometimes does the same like airport or television, the latter being a prefix and root word, the whole word meaning far seeing.

The forts or safe harbor squares were given as URUZ - ᚾ and FEHU - ᚠ, strong wishes or strong money or strong properties, by the sea captain. In looking at the meanings of the runes, I felt a more appropriate grouping would be URUZ - ᚾ and WUNJO - ᛒ, strong clan banner, or URUZ - ᚾ and OTHALA - ᛉ, strong clan house. I chose to use URUZ - ᚾ and WUNJO - ᛒ on my board since the clan banner can fly over any territory or village of the clan, but the clan house is normally the traditional home of the beginning of the clan, and there is only one. Also, FEHU - ᚠ is a plan or wish while WUNJO - ᛒ is a joy of an accomplishment.

The shoals were given BERKANO - ᛒ and SOWHILO - ᛋ, protection and victory, while the ignominious defeat was represented by URUZ - ᚾ and SOWHILO - ᛋ, strong victory. Both of these seem to be the reverse of what the square represents, a disruption in planned and orderly life which sends you back to start a new cycle. That is the meaning given to HAEGEL - ᚺ or HAGALAZ (its the beginning HHAA sound that is important in the naming of this rune). Even though this rune is used in the casting sticks, I also placed it on the board in the square of reversals since a shipwreck and a defeat are both considered a disaster beyond our control, or a reversal of fortune where fate takes a hand in the plans of men.

The runes I chose for the box to keep the pieces in was BERKANO - ᛒ, ING - ◇, and WUNJO - ᚹ representing Asgaard and/or Valhalla. The interpretation of these show the land (WUNJO - ᚹ) of the gods (BERKANO - ᛒ and ING - ◇) or as we know it, Asgaard. Breaking down Berkano to its components, as in a bind rune, we find SOWHILO - ᛋ and LAGUR - ᛚ. We can have the meaning of the flow or path of success to the land of ING - ◇. Since there is no rune for Odhin, ING - ◇ is substituted.

In a graduate level course at the university I attended, over twenty adults sat around and played games for credit. In the course of study we learned that games have been around as long as mankind, that in addition to tools for learning as children, games have served to model reality for adults. Chess is well over 2000 years old and a tool to teach strategy. The inclusion of DER WIKINGER as a separate chapter is precisely for its design as a model of the world view of those who went a Viking for fame and fortune. Many of the players marvel at the simplicity of the game, yet it still is a model for those living today as a way to understand life.

Chapter 8: THE ROOTS OF MAGIC

PHYSICS, QUANTUM PHYSICS, AND METAPHYSICS

This book was divided into eight chapters with a point in mind. The Northern tribes were one of the few ancient people who recognized a power in the number eight in their myths. Odhin's horse in the wild hunt has eight legs. Most of the other peoples myths included the first five prime numbers: one, two, three, five, and seven. Eight is the number of the periodic table in chemistry, of the perfect, full, electron shell. A fitting place to end.

All through this book we discussed the runes from a magical view and related this view to quantum theory tying the two together in the psyche. To many this could still seem tenuous to the extreme, like an electron about to convert to a photon. Yet it is precisely that jump which differentiates classical physics from quantum theory. The jump that transforms solid matter to wave form energy.

The view of mankind's ordinary reality can be called an ordinary or normal state of consciousness, similar to classical physics. When an individual enters an altered state of consciousness, it is similar to moving to the activities where quantum physics' laws apply. It does not negate the validity of the rules of classical physics, but quantum physics covers those situations not covered in classical or which seem to violate the rules of classical physics.

The drawing on the following page shows that science and magic are two faces of the same coin with religion the edge that separates them for most people. Both sides deal with rules for identifying and manipulating reality, but due to the influence of the church in the middle ages, only one has the blessing of acceptance. Astrology became astronomy and alchemy became chemistry when the aspects of the non-physical were removed to obtain the blessings of the church. Rather, I should say that these aspects were removed to not be condemned by the church as heresy and work of the devil. For many centuries science still was not blessed or accepted by the church, and many scientists who dared to propose theories against the church's doctrine were excommunicated.

If you look at the edge of a coin, you will see that edge, religion, and one of the two sides of the coin. Throughout history, religion would side with one face you can see, while ignoring the other. If you take the Christian religion as an example, it is siding with Science as it has since the late middle ages. At the same time, Christianity denies magic saying all magic is the work of the devil unless it is the magic that is performed by the priests and sanctioned by the Vatican. The edge of the coin is the form of the sacred circle, eternally without beginning or end, while the faces are planes that are bounded by this edge. This is a one dimensional and blindfolded view.

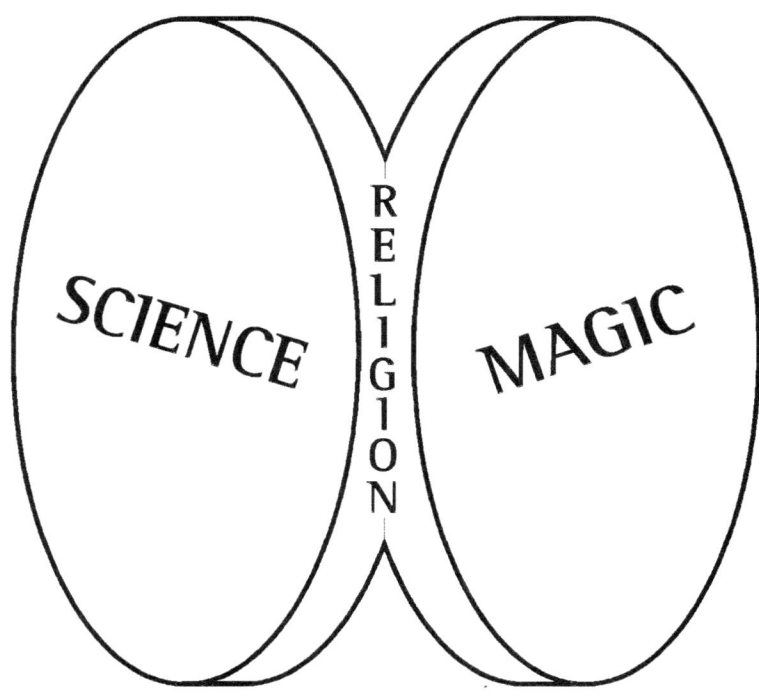

Science is blindfolded by the logic that it treats as a god, requiring an objective distancing between the observer and the event. If the scientist observer is thought to violate that distance, the fools of science think the entire observation is invalidated. This is not true. In reality, the only true requirements that the rules of science require is the experiment be observable, repeatable by others, and describable.

The Australian penny I use in this simile has three sides. The head on one side of the coin represents the logic of science. The kangaroo on the obverse is the magic of nature. The edge which is religion has the smallest area, yet it contains the other two defining what they can be.

Hold the coin firmly in your fist. There is more to it than just three sides, just as there is more to reality than magic, or science, or religion. There is more to the coin than each of them alone, and each of them together. There is a weight to the coin, not just a surface. There is a mass to the coin. While the three types of thought define reality, they still miss the reality below the surface. The material of the coin is a metallic matrix of one or more type of atoms. There is a similar pattern to reality, a similar way for things to fit together, a way they form a solid object.

Hold the coin with one edge on the table. Flick the edge of the coin with your finger causing it to spin. As it spins, the three sides disappear, becoming a one sided sphere. This shows the reality of the matrix of the coin, a glimpse of how religion, magic, and science are really just different ways of looking at reality.

Science strives to manipulate the matrix by hitting or pushing the atoms so one changes the other, or sets it free to be grabbed and manipulated by itself. It is set up for instant gratification. Magic recognizes the pattern, then gently strums the pattern like a guitar string, with the vibration causing a shift in the pattern. Most religions totally ignore the matrix, trying to describe the coin by how large the circle is while not taking into account either of the faces.

If it were not for the dividing edge of religion which flattens out the sphere, both science and magic would realize that they are only halves of a sphere. That they are only different ways of seeing and manipulating the matrix of reality.

Every good story has a point. The lesson of the coin is that being is existence. Existence is subjective, not objective. You cannot separate religion from science, science from magic, or magic from religion. You cannot separate yourself from the pattern, since you are a part of the pattern of existence, just as the pattern is a part of the creator.

You can make music by striking a hide with a stick as in a drum. This is the way of science. You can make music by stroking the strings with a horsehair feather as in a violin. This is the way of magic. Or you can make music by blowing in a hollow tube as in a flute. This is the way of religion. When all play the same tune at the same time you have the symphony of existence. When all three come together in metal you have a coin to buy a meal or a flower.

Shortly after explaining the coin, the compilation of essays in *Humanity* came to me. In it, the Catholic priest and Oblate of the de Sales order had a few essays on the dichotomy of science and religion. He propounded that the first shuns belief while the second shuns reason. His conclusion was that to see the big picture of how reality really is you need to use both.

The teachings of the schools are of science and reason. When an event occurs that does not fall within the neat and orderly rules and theories of science, it gets dismissed as the wanderings of a demented or unbalanced mind. When someone state a fact that counters the belief of a religion, that person is either deluded or the pawn of the devil. When belief and reason unite to work in accordance with the cosmic laws of creation, we call it magic.

This is like the argument between classical and quantum physics, both sides are right, it is just the view of the observer that changes. Science applies an artificial limitation of objectivity to its theorems while the metaphysical, or magical, view recognizes that reality is subjective in that each person receives the information through the filters of the senses and then translated in the symbolism needed for processing by the mind. Most people have an agreement on reality brought about by language and culture which gives the objectivity that science demands.

A redefinition of objectivity that is proposed by the sociologists and anthropologists examining shamans could be stated as *a consensus of observers on the happening of an event.* In studying shaman's trances, the only way they had to **observe** it was to participate in the trance. They could not have the clinical separation expected, but **repetition by others** yielded the same or very similar results. Therefore the experiments were repeatable, observable, and quantifiable in the **consensus** of the observers.

So we have a spectrum of physics which goes from classical physics to quantum physics to metaphysics. Each higher level recognizes the validity of the laws of the lower, but has a larger set which covers exceptions to the laws of the previous sets.

The mind of mankind with its ability to process and manipulate symbols, and so switch states of consciousness is the basis and the root of magic. Magic being the ability to interpret and manipulate reality by means outside the set of laws recognized by contemporary science. The researchers are just beginning to verify what the Shaman told them for centuries. Such as the existence of the aura which surrounds the human body and that the bark of the yew tree is good for curing some forms of disease. By altering their state of consciousness, the shaman's aura or bioelectrical field interacted with that of the yew and discovered the benefits of the bark, just like two computers talking via a modem.

In the magical view, coincidence or luck is just the working of the universe. The mind manipulates the symbols, puts out the request for an event to occur. Through proper visualization, the mind accesses the symbols and the bioelectric aura transmits the request out to the universe. Other entities can pick this up, interpret this into symbolism valid for them, process it, and set up the coincidences to fill the request if they concur. This can be other people in this existence, the super conscious of the planet, or the divine creator. The runes are a shorthand or symbolism that can be used for this.

Therefore, any combinations of actions which are designed to produce luck, coincidence, or synchronicity and bring about an event in the environment of an individual can be considered magical. The basis of almost all forms of magic is a visualization of the desired result, or a statement of the result verbally since not everyone is visually oriented. If this is considered, over 90% of the self-improvement and inspirational speakers are really teaching a course of MAGIC 101. But considering the stigma attached to magic in this culture these upstanding instructors call it anything and everything else.

MASTERS OF SPIRIT MAGIC

What are the ties between the runes and shamanism? In following the trails of the runes I have been using the bibliographies for the sources of some of the comments seen in my references and back tracked to see what was culled out of the books referenced. In several, the trails began to converge back to the same books, yet some parts were used and others ignored. There have been several others who noted the correspondences between the definitions of the shaman and some of the northern gods and heroes.

To put the cart before the horse, Odhin matches the parameters of shamanism in six ways:

1) Initiation of hanging on the Yggdrasil to find the runes.
2) His horse, Sleipnir, has 8 hooves as does the horses of Siberian, Murian, and Japanese shaman.
3) Renowned ability as a shape changer.
4) Necromancer, consulting the spirits of the dead.

5) Two familiars, the crows or ravens named Huginn (thought) and Muninn (memory) which bring information from the four corners of the world.
6) Use of Seidhr, a form of sorcery to foresee the future, normally the realm of women, taught to him by Freya.

Getting back to the horse, let us study the primary definitions of shamanism. The primary criteria of a shaman according to Mircea Eliade is conducting work in a trance or an altered state of consciousness, which could be a dream. Many of the exploits of Odhin could be considered recounting of work in such a state. The initiations of a shaman normally consist of a near death or death experience which has the effect of destroying the fear of death in the shaman. The shaman is the one to deal with matters of the spirit, both in dis-spirited illnesses, and in discourse with the spirits of deceased people. The major aids in shaman's work are spirits, both the aiding spirits commonly called familiars, and tutelary spirits which give advice and instruction. The last truly outstanding parameter for the shaman is knowledge of the secret languages including the ability to mime animals or take the form or persona of animal species.

The persona of the animal is sometimes accomplished through the use of a mask and ritual dance. The mask acts both to hide the person wearing it, and to project the aspect of the animal. This is another tool or technique of the shaman. One of the leading retro-heathen scholars prefers not to speak too directly on dangerous topics such as the runes, shamanism, and Odhin. As a safety device, Odhin gave the runes masks before releasing them to mankind. In this way, only those with the courage and integrity to wear the masks of the runes as a shaman wears an animal mask can learn the spirit behind the mask of the rune.

In a way these parameters also defined the duties of the shaman. The first and main duty was to consort with the spirits and ensure the dead were able to reach the land of the dead so they did not stay around and torment the living. The second duty in many cases was to use aid of familiar spirits to cure illnesses in people. Finally, the shaman was a fortune teller, either using the aid of the spirits, or to travel in his spirit body to find game for the hunters, lost spirits, or appropriate weather for hunting or travel.

There are six sorts of illnesses that are recognized in some shaman's tribes:
1) Accidents
2) Breach of taboo

3) Terror by monsters
4) Bad blood
5) Poisoning by sorcerers
6) Loss of the soul

The sex of the majority of shaman was dependent on tribe and country. In some locales the shaman were predominately male, in others female. In some locales such as Borneo the shaman were neither or both, being men living as women or vice versa. In all cases it is the ability to handle the altered states of consciousness that determined the individual that was to become a shaman. This ability to make the jump to an altered state of consciousness is the same sort of ability described in the previous section of this chapter, that of ordinary reality to magic or metaphysical reality.

In many places in this discourse I have made references to the Goddesses, not just of the Norse pantheon, but in relation to other Goddess worshipping religions. In most, the Goddess in known as the triple Goddess, having three names for the three stages of the woman's life. First is the maiden, normally considered pre-puberty, as could be represented by LAGUR - ſ, or virginal as represented by KENAZ - <, both of these being the end of the stage. The second stage is BERKANO - ß, or the Mother and Wife, the lover and pregnant woman who gives back life. The final stage is that of the crone, the post menopausal woman who can no longer conceive.

This crone is normally considered the typical witch, consorting with the spirits of the dead, brewing herbal potions, and making prophecies while in trance. Doesn't this sound a bit like the list of attributes for being a shaman? In many aspects, the third stage of the Goddess, called the crone, is very much like being a shaman. This is the time of the wise woman, the witch, the time of the spirit, and spirit magic. Some consider the best rune for this as HAEGEL - H, while some consider the WYRD -   as a better match. If you are a woman and the change is frightening due to the loss of your identity as a mother, HAEGEL - H is a good choice for menopause. But if you look forward to helping your sisters give birth, working with medicinal herbs, and learning the ways of the spirit, the WYRD -   may be a bit more appropriate.

Shifting focus a bit, in the description of WYRD -   , I began to weave the shaman into the runes. Not only does the crone have this same aspect of death and rebirth in working with the spirits as does the shaman, but she also has the aspects of the wise woman, a healer and a midwife, just as the shaman is a healer. The mysteries of death and divination are also in the province of both of these two forms of the spirit masters.

Dealing with the spirit plane necessarily means dealing with the aura and other manifestations of the astral body. The shaman normally makes an astral journey in healing, sometimes to remove foreign vibrational frequencies from the aura; frequencies the shaman senses as invading spirits of insects, plants, or minerals that have made their way past the person's guardian spirits.

In a way, this is a similar talent as being an empath, the ability to merge auras and sharing feelings and emotions. Just a different way of doing it, by feel instead of sight. Almost everyone experiences some form of this merging of the aura during sexual intercourse, falling in love, or just being room mates with someone for a long period of time.

For many people, the psychic abilities are strengthened and develop new manifestations with the coming of puberty. In women, it is strengthened further in pregnancy where they develop strong ties with their unborn child. These ties are used during life to safeguard the child. The majority of the men not called to the way of the shaman, never develop these skills and abilities. The majority of the women are too tied up with being mothers to develop them. It is only those women after menopause, and those men and women called to the spiritual way of the shaman that work to become the masters of the spirit magic in life.

THE MAGIC IN SONG

The heroes of the Kalevala were not mighty warriors of the blade, but the magicians of creation, and the magic used was song. I said rune notes in the first introduction to the Kalevala for both a pun on pronunciation, and for a connection. To explain the connection, I will need to describe the basic form of their song magic. Every hero had a slightly different talent, and so the magic proceeded a bit differently.

Each magician would start with a bit of matter, except for the creator of the universe who is so powerful that the song formed the matter. Each hero then formed the image in both mind and song of the completion of the magic work.

The smith would use forge and fire with his song; the minstrel his voice and kantele; and the rogue his charm as he sang of the transformation of the matter. Now, the ordinary, smaller magic was accomplished with word and verse telling a story of the transformation to be performed. The great minstrels and heroes did their greatest magical work with just tones or notes, the most powerful tones being inaudible to the human ear.

As an example, the weather witches could whistle up a storm or whistle away the clouds to let the sun shine, and these were not the most powerful or talented of the magicians. In a culture such as Chinese, the intonation of the word is vital to the meaning of the word. Edred Thorsson has a chant of the rune's sound, but the tone to go with the sound has been lost when the runes usage declined.

Further reading on the track of the Kalevala found information on the Finnish magic in the notes of the translator, W. F. Kirby. He found that the Finns, the Russians, and several others in the area of Siberia had a common magical belief. The sorcerers and magicians of these areas where the runes were found had a practice of making animals out of stumps and branches and moss. He pointed out that the magicians had to use materials to sing into another form in their magic. This even goes for the weather witches; feathers from a goose are turned into a snowstorm, and winds are whistled up, turning the breath into wind.

The point I am trying to stress here is that the magician provides the control on the creation of the desired result, the form of the result, but does not create the matter. Except for the creator of everything, Jumala, no magician in the Finnish songs could control the power needed to bring matter into existence.

There were a few other points of interest in the Kalevala not directly relating to magic in song from an anthropological point of study. We are dealing with stories from the times of the runes which show how the people viewed life and the magic which filled the world.

One item which goes back to the beginning of the book is that writing and reading is not mentioned in the Kalevala. The use of symbols to represent language was not universal to all cultures and people. Even at the time of Charlemagne of France, he, the king, could read, but he could not write. He had scribes to write his laws, write his proclamations and to copy books for him.

Another point of general interest deals with the power of the number three. In most instances actions are repeated three times for effect. The heroes are queried three times, they lie with the first two answers and reveal the truth with the third query. When spells or curses are pronounced, they are given a strength of three in a form unique in my study. The first invocation for a curse or spell is from the hero or his adversary, the second states that if that does not suffice, the power of some major spirit will be invoked to force the issue, finally if that spirit does not suffice to obtain the desired result, the power of Ukko or Jumala, the lord or creator of everything will be invoked. Sometimes even the magical songs are started three times, the first two times interruptions distracting the singer.

A maxim of magic states that it is wise to use only the minimal amount of force or energy to achieve one's goal. This is pointed out again and again and again in the stories of Kullervo and in the descriptions of items. The items which are deemed best are not the smallest, nor the largest, but those of middle stature. These are the ones of potent magical properties. Time and again Kullervo asks if he should do all he is capable of or if he should do acts of the middle force. He is told to do his manly best in almost all cases and so he ruins what he works on due to his incredible strength. He threshes the wheat and barley into chaff and dust, he rows so hard he breaks the oarlocks and ribs of the boat, and when he fishes with a net he pulls so hard the nets are shredded into pieces and the fish in it are diced into small fragments. It is only when the wise minstrel, Vainamoinen, is asked such a question is the reply to do just that which is needed to get the job done.

With that thought, all that needs to be said on using runes in light of today's psychology and physics has been said. The rest is up to you and your subconscious. May the song of your life be filled with harmony.

RUNIC STATES

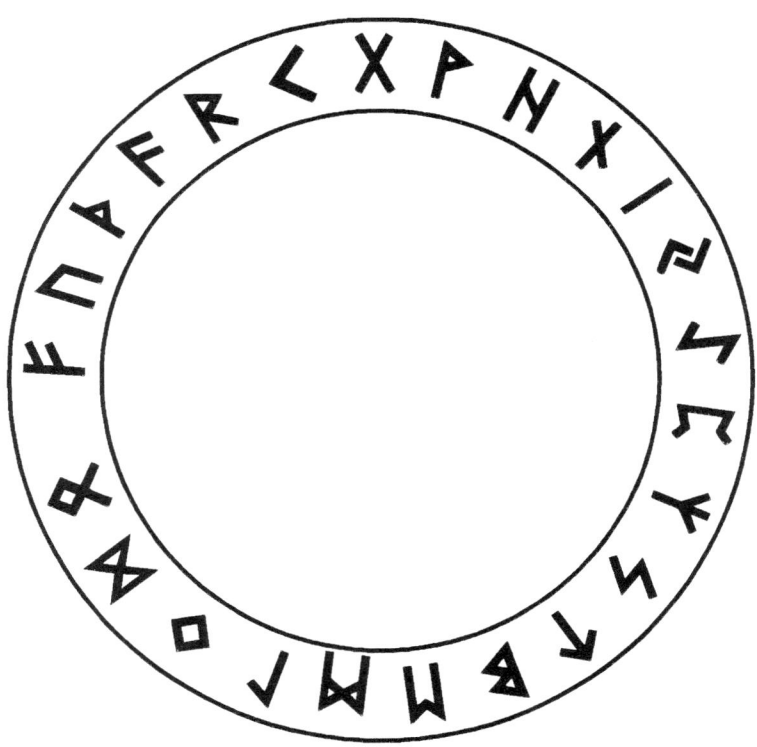

RUNIC STATES

BIBLIOGRAPHY

Applied IR Photography by Kodak. Published in 1970 by Kodak of Rochester, New York.

Astrological Thesaurus, Book 1, House Keywords by Michael Munkasey. Published in 1993 by Llewellyn Publications of St. Paul, Minnesota.

The Body Electric by Thelma Moss, PhD. Published in 1979 by J. P. Tarcher, Inc. of Los Angeles, California.

The Book of Rune Cards by Ralph Blum. Published in 1989 by St. Martin's Press of New York.

Cosmic Conflict by Mrs. E. G. White. Published in 1988 by Review & Herald Publishing of Washington, DC.

The Four Winds A Shaman's Odyssey into the Amazon by Alberto Villoldo and Erik Jendresen. Published in 1990 by Harper & Row of San Francisco, California.

FUTHARK A Handbook of Rune Magic by Edred Thorsson. Published in 1985 by Samuel Weiser, Inc. of York Beach, Maine.

Humanity by Fr. Hugh J. McKenna. Published in 1993 by Vantage Press of New York, New York.

John Bartlett's Familiar Quotations, 14th edition. Published in 1968 by Little, Brown, and Company of Boston, Massachusetts.

Kalevala, The Land of Heroes by W. F. Kirby. Published in 1985 by The Athlone Press of Dover, New Hampshire.

Land of Heroes, A retelling of the Kalevala by Ursula Synge. Published in 1978 by Fairfield Graphics of Fairfield, Pennsylvania.

Language: Mirror, Tool, and Weapon by George W. Kelling. Published in 1975 by Nelson Hall, Inc. of Chicago, Illinois.

Life Force, The Secret of Empowerment by Leo F. Ludzia. Published in 1987 by Llewellyn Publications of St. Paul, Minnesota.

Norse Gods and Giants by Ingi and Edgar Parin d'Aulaire. Published in 1967 by Doubleday & Company, Inc. of Garden City, New York.

The Old Norse Sagas by Halvdan Koht. Published in 1931 by W. W. Norton & Company of New York.

Pristine Yi King by Louis Culling. Published in 1989 by Llewellyn Publications of St. Paul, Minnesota.

The Reluctant Shaman by Kay Cordell Whitaker. Published in 1991 by Harper Collins Publishers of San Francisco, California.

Shamanism, Archaic Techniques of Ecstasy by Mircea Eliade. Published in 1974 by Princeton University Press.

SHON'JIR by C. J. Cherryh. Published in 1979 by Daw Books of New York, New York.

Star Wars by George Lucas. Produced in 1977 by Twentieth-Century Fox Film Corporation.

Tao Te Ching by Lao Tsu, translated by Gia-Fu Feng and Jane English. Published in 1972 by Alfred A. Knopf, Inc. of New York.

Tesla: Man out of Time by Margaret Cheney. Published in 1981 by Dell Publishing of New York, New York.

Urban Shaman by Serge Kahili King. Published in 1990 by Simon & Schuster of New York.

Viking Long Boats by Margaret Mulvihill. Published in 1989 by Glouchester Press of New York, New York.

The Viking Explorers by Rebecca Stefoff. Published in 1993 By Chelsea House Publishers of New York, New York.

A Viking Sailor by Christopher Gibb. Published in 1986 by Rourke Enter, Inc of Vero Beach, Florida.

The Viking World by Jaqueline Simpson. Published in 1980 by St. Martin's Press of New York, New York.

The Vikings by Hazel Martell. Published in 1986 by Warwick Press of New York, New York.

The Vikings by Robin Place. Published in 1985 by The Cambridge University Press.

The Vikings by Else Roesdahl. Published in 1987 by the Penguin Press of New York, New York.

The Way of the Shaman by Michael Harner. Published in 1982 by Bantam Books of New York, New York.

Webster's 3rd New International Dictionary. Published in 1971 by G & C Merriam Co. of Springfield, Massachusetts.

Webster's New World Dictionary 2nd College Edition. Published in 1982 by Simon & Schuster of New York.

When God Was A Woman by Merlin Stone. Published in 1976 by Harcourt Brace Jovanovich, Publishers of New York.

RUNIC STATES

GLOSSARY

a-Viking	The journey of trade or plunder of the Germanic tribes from which the word Viking derives.
ANSUR - ᚠ	The fourth rune. The rune of inspiration.
Asgaard	Dwelling place of the Norse Gods and Goddesses.
ash	A tree.
astral	Dealing with the astral plane or body, the spirit.
aurochs	The wild oxen of Europe, an aspect of URUZ - ᚾ.
Balder	The Norse God of light and peace.
banner	A flag or pennant, such as that of a clan or king.
bce	Functionally equivalent to BC, the term bce is a contraction for "Before Current Era", or "Before Christian Era".
BERKANO - ᛒ	The eighteenth rune; the Earth Goddess.
bind rune	A symbol combining the properties of two or more runes.
birch	A tree. An aspect of BERKANO - ᛒ.
Blum	Ralph Blum. Author of books on the runes.
Borr	Father of Odhin.
Brifrost	Rainbow bridge connecting Asgaard and Midgaard.
ce	A term functionally equivalent to AD, ce is a contraction for "Current Era" or "Christian Era".
chakra	An aspect of SOWHILO - ᛋ, junction of energy lines in the astral body.
conscious	Part of the mind that handles daily activities.
cunning	Aspect of ANSUR - ᚠ, deceitful or sly, quick of wit.
DAGAZ - ᛞ	The twenty-third rune. Rune of day and polarity.
dance	An aspect of RAIDHO - ᚱ. Rhythmic movement to music.
darkness	An aspect of WYRD - . Absence of light.
defense	An aspect of EIHWAR - ᛇ. Guarding against attack.
destiny	An aspect of WYRD - . Preordained fate.
EHWAR - ᛗ	The nineteenth rune. The rune of marriage.
EIHWAR - ᛇ	The thirteenth rune. The rune of the yew tree.
ELHAR - ᛉ	The fifteenth rune. The rune of life and health.
elk	An aspect of ELHAR - ᛉ, the rune of life.
energy	The difference in potentials. An aspect of force.

FEHU - ᚠ	The first rune. The rune of expansion and money.
fire	The act of burning. An aspect of KENAZ - ᚲ.
flow	Move like water in a stream. An aspect of LAGUR - ᛚ.
force	The four basic forms of potential in physics.
Freya	Norse Goddess of love and beauty.
Freyr	Norse God of fertility.
Futhark	The runic alphabet.
GEBO - X	The seventh rune. The rune of gifts and weddings.
Germanic	Those tribes and languages that diverged from a common stock that occupied the area where the majority of runic artifacts were located.
gestation	The period of pregnancy. An aspect of ING - ◊.
Ginnungagap	The chasm of the *Eddic* creation myth.
HAEGEL - ᚺ	The ninth rune. The rune of disruption.
HAGALAZ	An alternate spelling for HAEGEL - ᚺ.
harmony	Agreement of feelings and actions, an aspect of EHWAR - ᛗ.
Heimdall	Norse God, guardian of the rainbow bridge.
hope	Expectation. An aspect of WUNJO - ᚹ.
horse	A domestic animal. Base symbol of EHWAR - ᛗ.
hospitality	Ethical treatment of guests. An aspect of GEBO - X.
Huginn	Raven familiar of Odhin whose name means thought.
ING - ◊	The twenty-second rune. The Earth Father.
initiation	Ceremony of entry to a group; an aspect of PERTHO - ᛈ.
inspiration	A sudden brilliant idea; an aspect of ANSUR - ᚠ.
ISA - I	The eleventh rune. The rune of ice and stillness.
JERA - ᛃ	The twelfth rune. The rune of the yearly harvest.
justice	Fairness; an aspect of TIWAR - ↑.
Kalevala	The collection of Finnish folk tales.
kantele	A stringed musical instrument in the Kalevala.
KENAZ - ᚲ	The sixth rune. The rune of fire and lust.
Kullervo	The unlucky death/vengeance hero of the Kalevala.
LAGUR - ᛚ	The twenty-first rune. The rune of water flowing.
leek	A mild onion like vegetable; an aspect of LAGUR - ᛚ.
Loki	Norse God of cunning, trickery and deceit.

Magni	Norse God of strength, son of Thor.
mandala	A visual meditation aid.
MANNAZ - ᛗ	The twentieth rune. The rune of mankind.
marriage	A close union between two people; aspect of EHWAR - ᛗ.
Midgaard	The middle kingdom of the *Edda*, the earth.
Mjollnir	Thor's mighty hammer, "The Flashing Crusher"
money	A means to measure wealth, an aspect of FEHU - ᚠ.
moon	Aspect of WYRD - , a satellite that orbits a planet.
Muninn	A raven familiar of Odhin whose name means memory.
NAUDHIR - ᚾ	The tenth rune. The rune of a strong compulsion.
oak	A tree.
Odhin	The chief of the Norse Gods, father and war chief.
opening	An aspect of KENAZ - ᚲ, removal of obstructions.
OTHALA - ᛟ	The twenty-fourth rune; the rune of the clan house.
pattern	A design for creating something, aspect of URUZ - ᚢ.
perseverance	Sticking to a purpose
PERTHO - ᛈ	The fourteenth rune. The rune of predestination.
possessions	Material goods. An aspect of FEHU - ᚠ.
prayer	A request, an aspect of FEHU - ᚠ.
predestination	A belief that the course of your life is set at or before your birth.
primal	First or fundamental, the base derivative.
prosperity	Possessing wealth, an aspect of OTHALA - ᛟ.
protection	Keeping safe from harm, an aspect of HAEGEL - ᚺ.
Ragnarok	The final battle of the Gods in the *Edda*.
RAIDHO - ᚱ	The fifth rune. The rune of the journeys.
rebirth	Reincarnation. An aspect of BERKANO - ᛒ.
regeneration	To replace what is lost, an aspect of SOWHILO - ᛋ.
runecast	Any method of divination with runes.
sacrifice	To make sacred by offering for a deities use.
Seidhr	A form of divination from the *Edda*.
sensuality	Pleasing to the senses; aspect of KENAZ - ᚲ.
shaman	A person dealing with the spirit world.
shamanism	The practices of dealing with the spirits.
Shon'Jir	A game teaching acceptance of your life.
Sleipnir	The eight legged horse of Odhin.

SOWHILO - ᛋ	The sixteenth rune. The rune of the sun.
subconscious	A part of the mind dealing with dreams and memory.
superconscious	The part of the mind dealing with deities.
swan	A bird. An aspect of ELHAR - ᛉ.
synchronicity	Fortuitous happenings when in time with reality.
synergy	When the whole is greater than the sum of the parts.
Thor	The Norse god of storms and weddings.
thorn	A stiff, protective leaf of a plant, aspect of THURISAR - ᚦ.
Thorsson	Edred Thorsson, an author of texts on the runes.
THURISAR - ᚦ	The third rune. The rune of directed energy.
TIWAR - ᛏ	The seventeenth rune. The rune of jurisprudence.
torch	A method of creating light. An aspect of KENAZ - ᚲ.
transition	The state of movement between two points. An aspect of EHWAR - ᛗ.
Tyr	Norse god of war and justice. An aspect of TIWAR - ᛏ.
Ukko	The great creator of the *Kalevala*.
unconscious	The state of the mind below the subconscious.
URUZ - ᚢ	The second rune. The rune of the ox.
Vainamoinen	The central hero, great minstrel and shaman of the Kalevala.
Valhalla	The hall of fallen heroes in Norse mythology.
Valkyrie	The daughters of Odhin who help him collect fallen heroes from the field of battle for Valhalla.
vectors	Means to measure force including direction of force and amount of force.
victory	Success in battle. An aspect of TIWAR - ᛏ.
Vidar	Norse God; patron of kings, and governors.
Viking	Traders and raiders of the Germanic tribes.
Void	The vast nothingness from which everything springs.
Wikinger	German for Viking. The game found in the Viking graves.
wisdom	Knowledge and good judgment. An aspect of URUZ - ᚢ.
Wotan	The chief of the Norse Gods, Odhin.
WUNJO - ᚹ	The eighth rune. The rune of joy and fellowship.
WYRD -	The rune of zero, and fate. Old English for fate.
yew	A tree. An aspect of EIHWAR - ᛇ ruling communication.
Yggdrasil	The tree that supports the worlds in the *Edda*.
Ymir	The first giant found in the ice of creation.

INDEX

A-Viking 27, 43, 53, 99, 172
ANSUR . . v, 27, 28, 37-40, 43, 46, 55, 62, 71, 85, 107, 113, 121, 123, 124, 126, 127, 129, 136, 137, 149, 172, 173
Asgaard 34, 38, 39, 62, 138, 155, 172
Ash 70, 148, 152, 172
Astral 77-79, 82, 93, 94, 116, 118, 123, 128, 146, 147, 163, 172
Aurochs 30, 172
Balder 99, 172
Banner . . . . v, 49, 50, 87, 88, 94, 106, 114, 125, 128, 154, 172
BERKANO . . vi, 27, 28, 36, 55, 62, 71, 79, 81, 86-89, 97, 99, 100, 107, 117, 121-124, 126-129, 135, 136, 154, 155, 162, 172, 174
Bindrune 134, 135, 138
Birch 70, 86, 87, 89, 117, 136, 172
Blum . . . . ix, 3, 18, 21, 46, 121, 168, 172
Borr 99, 172
Brifrost 38, 93, 118, 123, 138, 172
Chakras 80, 82, 117
Conscious 2, 4, 70, 146, 160, 172
Cunning 61, 70, 74, 88, 99, 172, 173
DAGAZ . . . vi, 23, 55, 62, 82, 102, 103, 107, 119, 122, 123, 125, 127, 138, 172
Dance 40-43, 46, 113, 126, 161, 172
Darkness 20, 22, 23, 45, 82, 103, 112, 125, 172
Defense 12, 34, 36, 55, 69, 71, 116, 128, 172
Destiny 20, 21, 23, 57, 58, 112, 125, 172
EHWAR . . . . vi, 43, 48, 55, 59, 62, 79, 90-92, 107, 118, 122-126, 172-175
EIHWAR . . . . . vi, 36, 40, 62, 69-71, 79, 124, 126-128, 137, 139, 172, 175
ELHAR . vi, 36, 43, 59, 62, 71, 77-79, 92, 94, 116, 121, 123, 126-128, 172, 175
Elk 77, 78, 116, 172
Energy . . . 25-28, 31-36, 41, 42, 46, 49, 50, 57, 61, 62, 65, 82, 92, 96, 98, 100, 112-114, 118, 121, 129, 130, 136, 139, 156, 165, 172, 175
FEHU . . . . v, 25-28, 32, 36, 46, 55, 62, 107, 112, 121, 122, 124, 129, 130, 136, 154, 173, 174
Fire . . v, 1, 24, 30, 44-46, 61, 62, 66, 84, 87, 88, 106, 114, 130, 134, 163, 173

Force .. 1, 12, 22, 26, 29, 31, 32, 35, 36, 39, 58, 61, 71, 75, 78, 79, 95, 97,
         99, 103, 113, 118, 127, 129, 130, 140, 165, 169, 172, 173, 175
Freya 44-46, 66, 88, 114, 125, 126, 161, 173
Freyr 46, 64, 66, 100, 115, 125, 126, 173
Futhark 17, 18, 132, 144, 149, 168, 173
GEBO ...... v, 47, 48, 50, 62, 92, 103, 106, 114, 121, 124, 125, 138, 173
Germanic .. ix, 7, 11, 12, 24, 39, 42, 48, 57, 58, 62, 65-67, 74, 78, 81, 87,
                          89, 101, 152, 153, 172, 173, 175
Gestation 55, 98-100, 107, 118, 122, 123, 173
Ginnungagap 24, 30, 46, 62, 173
HAEGEL .... v, 19, 32, 36, 52-55, 57-59, 62, 71, 107, 115, 121, 122, 128,
                          130, 153, 154, 162, 173, 174
Hagalaz 19, 154, 173
Harmony 50, 62, 92, 106, 124, 136, 165, 173
Heimdall 93, 94, 118, 123, 138, 173
Hope 49, 65, 114, 173
Horse .... vi, 59, 79, 91, 92, 126, 156, 160, 161, 173, 174
Hospitality 47, 48, 114, 173
Ice ... vi, 1, 24, 30, 45, 46, 53, 55, 60-62, 87, 88, 115, 124, 126, 128, 173,
                                                                175
ING .. vi, 21, 32, 46, 55, 62, 66, 88, 98-101, 106, 107, 118, 121, 122, 124,
                          126, 127, 130, 135, 144, 149, 155, 173
Initiation 73, 116, 160, 173
Inspiration .... v, 37, 38, 55, 62, 71, 107, 113, 123, 172, 173
ISA .... vi, 1, 24, 31, 32, 45, 46, 55, 60-62, 82, 87, 88, 103, 115, 123, 124,
                          126, 128, 130, 136, 138, 139, 173
JERA ..... vi, 21, 24, 42, 46, 62, 64-67, 82, 100, 103, 115, 125-128, 173
Justice 83-85, 88, 99, 117, 173, 175
Kalevala 8-10, 45, 71, 96, 163, 164, 168, 173, 175
Kantele 163, 173
KENAZ ... v, 1, 21, 24, 32, 40, 43-46, 51, 55, 61, 62, 66, 87, 88, 103, 106,
         107, 114, 121, 122, 124-128, 130, 134, 136, 148, 162, 173-175
Kullervo 165, 173
LAGUR . vi, 1, 32, 46, 55, 61, 62, 70, 71, 79, 87, 88, 95, 97, 118, 121, 127-
                          130, 134-137, 149, 155, 162, 173
Leek 95-97, 118, 173
Loki 35, 37-39, 61, 67, 70, 71, 74, 113, 125, 126, 173
Magni 34, 174
Mandala .... ix, 19, 174
MANNAZ .... vi, 38, 50, 62, 79, 93, 94, 106, 107, 118, 121, 123, 125, 174
Marriage 45, 48, 90, 92, 118, 124, 172, 174
Midgaard 62, 125, 153, 172, 174

Mjollnir 33, 34, 113, 128, 174
Money 25, 27, 31, 32, 112, 120, 124, 135, 154, 173, 174
Moon 20-24, 66, 106, 112, 124, 139, 174
Muninn 138, 161, 174
NAUDHIR ... vi, 14, 43, 46, 51, 55-59, 61, 62, 79, 92, 106, 107, 115, 121, 122, 125, 126, 128, 130, 138, 139, 149, 174
Oak 18, 70, 132, 148, 152, 174
Odhin ... 9, 20, 22, 23, 35, 38-40, 45, 62, 67, 70, 71, 74, 84, 99, 112, 125, 137, 138, 149, 155, 160, 161, 172-175
Opening 44-46, 55, 82, 107, 114, 122, 174
Orlog 55, 57, 58, 62, 73, 74, 107, 116, 122, 125
OTHALA ... vi, 27, 32, 36, 50, 51, 55, 62, 71, 94, 100, 105-108, 119, 121-125, 128, 144, 154, 174
Pattern . ix, 3, 9, 19, 31, 32, 46, 54, 55, 57, 58, 61, 62, 107, 122, 123, 132, 134, 158, 174
Perseverance 30, 84, 85, 117, 174
PERTHO .... vi, 38, 51, 55, 57, 58, 62, 73-75, 87, 106, 107, 116, 122, 124, 125, 128, 173, 174
Possessions 25-27, 32, 43, 112, 124, 174
Prayer 25-28, 55, 62, 107, 112, 122, 123, 133, 136, 174
Predestination 74, 174
Primal 25-27, 32, 46, 52, 53, 60, 62, 73, 74, 112, 115, 116, 123, 130, 174
Prosperity 27, 32, 105, 106, 119, 124, 135, 174
Protection 15, 36, 52, 71, 78, 86, 115, 117, 128, 154, 174
Ragnarok 39, 99, 153, 174
RAIDHO .... v, 32, 40-43, 46, 51, 55, 59, 62, 79, 85, 87, 88, 92, 106, 107, 113, 122, 123, 126-128, 130, 136, 137, 147, 154, 172, 174
Rebirth 86-88, 100, 162, 174
Regeneration 44-46, 80, 81, 87, 88, 114, 117, 124, 136, 174
Runecast 4, 70, 132, 174
Sacrifice ... 30, 44, 45, 66, 83-85, 100, 114, 117, 123, 124, 148, 153, 174
Seidhr 161, 174
Sensuality 90, 91, 118, 125, 174
Shaman 9, 20, 22, 23, 26, 42, 66, 67, 75, 76, 112, 134, 137, 159-163, 169, 170, 174, 175
Shamanism 9, 39, 67, 70, 71, 140, 160, 161, 169, 174
SHON'JIR 20, 23, 112, 169, 174
Sleipnir 160, 174
SOWHILO .... vi, 32, 35, 46, 50, 58, 62, 80-82, 85, 87, 88, 103, 106, 117, 123-128, 130, 135, 136, 152, 154, 155, 172, 174, 175

Subconscious .... ix, 2-4, 19, 20, 23, 54, 57, 61, 70, 91, 95, 97, 112, 118, 120, 146, 165, 175
Superconscious 54, 70, 145, 146, 175
Swan 77-79, 116, 126, 175
Synchronicity 57, 73-75, 116, 128, 160, 175
Synergy 133, 175
Tao 3, 20, 112, 169
Thor 34, 35, 125, 126, 153, 174, 175
Thorn 33, 34, 113, 153, 175
Thorsson ...... ix, 3, 18, 19, 21, 26, 46, 71, 88, 134, 144, 164, 168, 175
THURISAR . v, 32-36, 46, 50, 61, 62, 71, 106, 113, 121, 122, 124, 126-128, 130, 175
TIWAR .... vi, 9, 40, 43, 62, 71, 82-85, 117, 121, 123, 124, 127, 137-139, 152, 173, 175
Torch 44-46, 51, 106, 114, 128, 148, 175
Transition 55, 90, 92, 107, 118, 122, 123, 147, 154, 175
Tyr 84, 85, 117, 175
Ukko 165, 175
Unconscious 2, 3, 23, 175
URUZ .. v, 27, 29-32, 46, 55, 57, 61, 62, 101, 107, 113, 121-124, 130, 154, 172, 174, 175
Vainamoinen 87, 165, 175
Valhalla 39, 152, 153, 155, 175
Valkyrie 39, 175
Vectors 33-35, 113, 175
Victory 39, 82-85, 117, 123, 139, 148, 152, 154, 175
Vidar 149, 175
Viking .... ix, 9, 11-14, 16, 23, 26, 27, 43, 53, 70, 99, 147, 149, 152, 155, 169, 170, 172, 175
Void 20, 22-24, 46, 61, 62, 112, 175
Wagon 30, 41-43, 51, 88, 92, 106, 113, 126, 128, 154
Wikinger .... vii, ix, 149, 152, 155, 175
Wisdom 20, 23, 29, 87, 112, 113, 137, 175
Wotan 99, 175
WUNJO .. v, 49, 50, 62, 87, 88, 92, 94, 106, 107, 114, 121, 124, 125, 128, 136, 138, 154, 155, 173, 175
WYRD .. v, 7, 14, 20, 22-24, 46, 58, 61, 62, 74, 82, 103, 112, 124-127, 132, 133, 162, 172, 174, 175
Yew 22, 69-71, 116, 137, 139, 152, 159, 160, 172, 175
Yggdrasil 71, 160, 175
Ymir 30, 31, 62, 63, 175